THE
Working Mom's Book

THE Working Mom's Book

OF HINTS, TIPS, AND EVERYDAY WISDOM

Louise Lague

Peterson's

Princeton, New Jersey

Visit Peterson's Education Center on the Internet (World Wide Web) at
http://www.petersons.com

Library of Congress Cataloging-in-Publication Data

Lague, Louise
    The working mom's book of hints, tips, and everyday wisdom.
        p. cm.
        ISBN 1-56079-461-5
        1. Working mothers—United States—Life skills guides.   2. Mothers—
Employment—United States. I. Title.
HQ759.48.L34   1995
646.7'0085'2—dc20   95-5094
                                                            CIP

Printed in the United States of America

10 9 8 7 6 5 4 3 2 1

Acknowledgments

Many thanks to Mary Kay Blakely, Janet Chan, Patti Donahue, Kathy Gorup, Lucy Hedrick, Carol Hupping, Ann Jackson, Bonnie Johnson, Joann Kaufmann, Janet Spencer King, Maurice and Elizabeth Lague, Michael Lutin, Sue Mittenthal, Ann Moore, Martha Nelson, Barbara Plumb, Lynn Ruane, Ned Scharff, Susan Seliger, Mary Simons, Richard B. Stolley, Barbara Tebay, Carrie Tuhy, and Sally Witte for their understanding, information, and encouragement.

For Ted and Alec, who made me a
working mom in the first place—
and so very much more.

Contents

CHAPTER ONE

Guilty, Guilty, Guilty!

On the first day that the "Today" show was broadcast from its glassed-in, sidewalk-side studio, Katie Couric admitted she felt guilty about not being able to go out and greet all the people who were pressing their noses against the glass.

"Of course," she added. "I feel guilty in every aspect of my life, so why not this one?"

Of course she feels guilty. She's a working mother. We all do.

The feeling of working mother guilt is this: You worry about home when you're at work, and you worry about work when you're at home.

You feel you are *always* in the wrong place, *always* doing the wrong thing.

This guilt mantra—if you let it chant within you—will become true soon enough, paralyzing you and making you feel what psychotherapists call *stuck*.

This uncomfortable feeling we have—this feeling that nothing is quite enough, that we are never quite at peace, that the bits of the puzzle don't all fit together—is not all about guilt.

Some of it is about trying to live up to the housekeeping standards of another generation, about being overstressed and undervalued, about leading a lonesome life in the midst of human racket, and about not rewarding ourselves.

In other parts of this book, we'll deal with all that. But first, let's do away with guilt.

♦ GETTING RID OF THE GUILTS

If you find no concrete evidence that you are being deficient as a mother or a worker, but you are still being haunted by this feeling of nonspecific guilt, then you should shoo it off before it takes hold like a tick.

You are now ready for the one and only foolproof

GUILT EXORCISM EXERCISE

First, sit down alone in a quiet place with a cup of tea. Then ask yourself this question: *Why am I working?*

- Do you have to do it for the money? Then you have no choice and cannot feel guilty.

- Are you working to give your kids a better life? Is it for braces, education, broadening travel, music camp? Then what's to feel guilty about?

- Is it to give yourself a better material life or maintain the same one? When you became a mother, were you already too old and spoiled to give up your own car, your vacation trips, and your dinners out? You deserve them more than ever now. There is no reason to feel guilty. Earn, enjoy the fruits of your labor, and share them with your children.

- Are you working because the activity itself makes you happy? This may be the best reason of all. Happy mothers make happy children. In all relationships, only when you are happy with yourself can you give anything of value to others.

Once you have thought this all out, if you have satisfied yourself that you have nothing to feel guilty about, forget about it once and for all. Guilt is a monumental waste of time.

◆ DO THE KIDS MIND, REALLY?

Last year our company sponsored a Take Our Daughters to Work Day. At lunch time, the girls left their mothers and fathers to eat together in the auditorium while they heard a panel of successful women discuss their careers. At one point, the moderator, Jane Pauley, asked the girls:

"How many of you have mothers who work?"

About 95 percent raised their hands.

"And how many of those wish their mothers *wouldn't* work?"

Now only about five percent raised their hands.

I was astounded. I knew that throughout this 47-story building, there were scores of working moms feeling riddled with guilt at this very moment, partly because they thought their kids didn't want them to work.

I wanted to run down through all the corridors and whoop and shout and shake them and say, "Girls! It's okay! It's okay! The kids don't mind at all!"

◆ LEST WE FORGET: YOUR JOB DOES GOOD THINGS FOR YOUR CHILDREN

Your children get a lot of good stuff out of your work. Not just the baseball caps with the company logo and the free samples of whatever you bring home.

They benefit from the tales you tell over dinner. They learn from the things you explain to them about what you do. They brag about you at school.

They learn that work is interesting, that it has dignity, that it is necessary and pleasing, and that it is a perfectly natural thing for both mothers and fathers to do.

Because your basic job as a parent is to prepare your children to conduct meaningful adult lives, one of your more valuable gifts to them will be to teach them the value, necessity, and joy of work.

Your work enriches your children more than it deprives them.

THE WORKING MOM MANTRA

I'm doing the best I can
Each place where I am
While I am there.

CHAPTER TWO

Quality Time

I once rode with a cab driver who had pictures of his four children, all in cap and gown, lined up on his dashboard. I told him it was a pretty impressive lineup.

"This one just graduated from high school and is going to college," he said. "This one is a junior in college. This one is a lawyer, and this one is in medical school," he said, puffing with pride.

"Wow," I said, "how did you do that?"

"We brought them to a different museum every Sunday," he said.

What the cab driver and his wife had accomplished had little to do with money, but it had much to do with quality time. Certainly they had no shortage of chores to do and television to watch, but instead they dropped everything and dragged the kids off to stimulate their minds and make them curious. At the same time, they bonded as a family. The children learned their parents' values and became people their elders could be proud of.

♦ QUALITY TIME IS REAL

Some people say quality time doesn't exist. They think it is something working parents invented to keep ourselves from feeling so guilty.

Nonsense. Anybody who knows the difference between the kind of conversation you have walking in the woods and the kind of conversation you have between the segments of a show on Nickelodeon can tell you that quality time exists.

Quality time is when you and your child are together and keenly aware of each other. You are enjoying the same thing at the same time, even if it is just being in a room or going for a drive in the car. You are somehow in tune, even while daring to be silent together.

You can have it with a baby or a child or a teenager or a grown-up offspring. And mothers who work can have just as much of it as mothers who don't.

This is because there are two kinds of quality time, planned and unplanned. Planned is the kind that is more likely to happen, and it is the one that mothers who work outside the home rely on most.

Quality time can be as elaborate as a trip abroad or as simple as come-here-and-help-me-wash-the-car. It can be a museum exploration trip, going out for ice cream, or staying home alone together with one delicious video and a bowl of popcorn. It can be a good talk on the way to the dry cleaners. It can be silence during a walk to view the sunset.

One-on-one is best, and all combinations work well. Girls only, boys' night out, mother-son lunches, father-daughter dinners. What is important is simply being together without distraction.

◆ EVENINGS BEYOND ARSENIC

All the way home each day, the working mother fantasizes about her triumphant return from the vineyards of hard labor to the warm, embracing bosom of her adoring family. Her children will meet her at the door with hugs and cheerful cries of "Mom's home!" The littlest will clutch her lovingly about the knees. She will slip into a silk caftan, accept a glass of chilled Chardonnay served from a silver tray by the butler, and settle by a roaring fire.

Her children surround her at the hearth, recounting the triumphs of the day. One has scored the winning home run at Little League; another has won the Latin prize. And the oldest has finally broken up with that hideous guy with the nose ring.

When Mom has exclaimed about all the good news, and perhaps finished counseling one child through a troubled moment, she rings a gong and they all repair to the dining room, where dinner is served.

In our dreams.

In fact, we all get home just in time for Arsenic Hour, that hideous abyss before dinner when blood sugar is low and everybody is crabby.

The kids are glued to the television. There's a stack of new bills in the mail. The phone rings. Dinner must be made. There are permission slips from school to sign. Homework needs finishing. A mom could crack up. Can there really *be* quality time?

Indeed. Because this is the only time you're going to see your children all day, you have every right to clear the space for Mega Quality Time. Take hold of this evening before it grinds you into a quivering mass of worn-out pulp, flopping into bed exhausted after having done a lot of ridiculous administrative things, not one of which was either Meaningful or Fun.

10 WAYS TO PUT QUALITY TIME INTO THE AVERAGE WEEKDAY EVENING

1. Change your clothes right away when you come home from work. Take off that tight, tired working-mom outfit and put on those leggings, that caftan, those shorts, the sweats. Symbolically, you're sloughing off the world of work and slipping into the unconstricted mode that's required to enjoy quality time.

2. Use the answering machine even if you're home. Arsenic Hour is the very moment that total strangers who cannot even pronounce your name call you, ask you how you are, and then try to sell you light bulbs.

Show no mercy. Remember, these people are deliberately targeting your evening. It is not a *coincidence* that they're calling at this hour of the day.

If you should accidentally answer a solicitation call, politely say: "I'm sorry, my family is sitting down to dinner now. If you would tell me what time *your* family sits down to dinner, I will call you back then."

If the machine collects messages from people you actually know and like, try to return as many as possible when it's convenient for *you*.

3. Be a total Tartar about your kids' time as well. Pre-plan so that when you get home, *they* are free to be with *you*. If you have a baby or a toddler at home with a sitter, for example, have the child fed and bed-ready before you arrive at home. Your little joy will be much cheerier—and cleaner to hug as well.

If you have school-age children, ask them to get their homework done before you get home, whether in an after-school program, with the aid of a sitter's nagging, or on their own.

Contrary to popular myth (one very effectively spread by a national secret underground network of third graders), parents are not actually supposed to do homework either *for* or *with* their children. The idea of homework is to reinforce what was learned during class time, and it involves only the child and the subject matter at hand. No parents need be involved.

The ideal is to ask them to finish everything before your return home from work, except for sticky, difficult, puzzling stuff that they *absolutely, positively, without a doubt* need help with. That final bit of help can be turned into quality time. (If, for some reason, your school-age child seems functionally incapable of starting or finishing any of his homework without you, something is wrong. Talk to the teacher.)

4. As much as possible, avoid cooking on weekday nights, unless it is a real source of relaxation for you. Pre-cook on the weekends, use microwaveable food, or order carry-out. Send out for pizza, pick up Chinese, boil pasta, open cans of soup. Save all sorts of fancy cooking for the weekend.

5. Never do kitchen work alone. Even if cooking is opening a can and cleaning up is tossing out the paper plates, have at least one child by your side to help you or talk to you, even if it's a baby in a seat or a two-year-old plopped on the counter. By the time they're four, they should be helping.

6. After dinner, don't give in to the temptation to just putter around, sift aimlessly through the mail, or move objects back to the rooms they belong in.

Instead, *do* something. Take one child tonight and another child tomorrow night, or get the family all together. Even if you only have half an hour before your children's bedtime, you can build a house of blocks, work on a jigsaw puzzle, stroll around the neighborhood, talk on the front stoop, walk the dog, clean the gerbil's cage, play cards, go out for ice cream.

These situations are all little Petrie dishes where conversations can grow.

7. Pick your arguments carefully *always*, but especially on weekday nights, when time is short. Try to avoid nagging and arguing.

While issues of safety, morality, and courtesy must be addressed immediately, try not to make dinner time and precious evening time all about "your-hideous-table-manners," "your-terrible-junk-food-habit," or "how-can-you-dress-like-that?"

If you have serious concerns about these things, save them for a special talk on the weekend so your child will know you're really serious and not just blowing off steam. Hold his hands, look in his eyes, and sandwich your message between pillows of praise for what he's doing right.

8. Read to your children at night for as many years as they'll put up with it. Bedtime reading promotes everything from cuddling to vocabulary to eventual discussions about ideas. Best of all, from the kids' point of view, reading in bed postpones bedtime.

Be equally unafraid of silly stories and great literature. Pick a book that you enjoy, too, and read with feeling. Start with *Pat the Bunny* and work your way up to *Treasure Island*.

9. Before sleep, reflect or pray together, but leave out that scary thing about "if I should die before I wake."

10. Resist the temptation to let the kids stay up late just because you haven't seen them all day. Get them to bed early enough to give you some adult time.

You need it, and they need to understand that your every waking hour cannot be devoted just to them.

◆ BUILDING BETTER WEEKENDS

I've never met a working mother who did not, at some point, come back to work after a weekend off, throw down her purse, flop in her chair with head tossed back and arms akimbo, and shriek, *"Thank God it's Monday!"*

While most people feel blue on Mondays, working mothers are often cheerful on Mondays, happy to be again free from minute-to-minute weekend meals, errands, chores, and family obligations.

To be perfectly frank, weekends can have a certain unattractive *emotional* tone as well.

Sometimes children are at their worst on weekends, because they've been good as gold at the day-care center or school all week and they've been saving their real feelings just for you.

Sometimes husbands are at their worst on weekends for exactly the same reason.

Sometimes we moms are no fun on weekends, because we've gone from scheduling our own weekday lives (meeting, gossip break, work, cruise through favorite clothing store, work, gym, work, lunch with funniest friend) to being at the mercy of everyone else's weekend schedule (karate class, auto tune-up, dinner at grandma's, groceries, piano recital, dry cleaning, church, play rehearsal).

The trouble with most weekends is that *duty comes first*, sometimes by necessity and sometimes by default.

Unfortunately, we tend to view the workweek, when we are at our jobs, as a time when we are *unable* to do what we historically, culturally, and foolishly believe to be a woman's *real* work, that is, household and family chores. Therefore, we have this ridiculous uncontrollable urge to make up for it on the weekends.

Sometimes we feel like we've been goofing off all week doing work that we really *like* to do, and now we have to pay for it by doing a lot of hideous, boring things. You know, the things that women are *supposed* to do.

Think this over and adjust this attitude immediately.

COMBINING UNAVOIDABLE CHORES WITH Q-TIME

One way to squeeze quality time into the weekend is to take the kids along on errands, preferably one at a time.

A toddler-burdened errand will of course take up to four times as long. Toddlers stop to poke and stare at *everything* along the way. An intelligent

◆ QUALITY TIME 911 ◆

There are evenings and some entire weekends when you wish you'd never come home at all. You were expecting warmth, support, cuddles, and surcease from worry. Instead you got temper tantrums, arguments, tears, and frustration.

No matter what the cause of anxiety, try to *give your family more love on the days they deserve it least.* This is not because you did something wrong yesterday to make them crabby and hateful today. It is because this is the day they need the stroking, the attention, the affection.

If you are very lucky, they will do the same for you when you need it most.

---

toddler can do up to ten minutes at a fire hydrant. ("Mmm. It's exactly my size. It's hard. It doesn't move. What the heck is this thing?")

Once you all finally get inside the grocery store, toddlers are notorious for pulling the bottom can out of displays, verbally *wanting*, and inevitably screaming to *get stuff* even at the no-candy register.

But take heart. There is good news up ahead on the shopping-with-kids front. By the time she's six, you can give her little assignments from the grocery list and have her hunt out things to bring back to your cart. When he's ten, you can wait in the car while he runs into the dry cleaner's, happy to be trusted with the chore and learning about the ways of human commerce at the same time.

Families with children can make entire field trips out of a Saturday's errands, alternating the fun ones with the routine and the places grown-ups like with the places kids like, and stopping for a snack in between.

But a simple day of errands can seem, to a child, like an around-the-world trip to a lot of tedious places on a train with very bad suspension. When a child—or an adult—gets bored, cranky, sleepy, and overwrought, bring him home.

WEEKEND WORDS TO LIVE BY:
LIST ERRANDS, BUT SCHEDULE FUN

Most of us conduct our weekends around the notion that chores come first, and if we finish them on time, we will all go to the movies . . . maybe, if

◆ DEATHBED PRIORITY TEST ◆

Weekend planning is a prime time to apply the Deathbed Priority Test: On your deathbed, will you wish you'd spent more prime weekend hours grocery shopping or walking in the woods with your kids?

---

we feel like it and we're not too tired and the baby isn't napping and it isn't too close to the time the big game starts on television.

Instead, try this next week: Scatter some of the chores into the weekdays and plan a day where a family date takes priority over everything else. Other errands and chores can be tucked in around it, if you have time, if you feel like it, if you're not too tired, and so forth.

Using your planned family date—ball game, family hike, museum trip, leaf raking, Monopoly game, dinner in a restaurant—as the central point of the day and then squeezing in errands around it will provide some glimmer of the pleasurable way weekends used to be before the kids came along.

The whole trick is to plan family fun as abundantly as family duty. That will go a long way toward actually making it happen.

♦ GET A (SOCIAL) LIFE!

I once knew a young woman so desperately guilty, so hopelessly enslaved to her children, that whenever another couple asked her and her husband out on a Saturday night, she refused.

Quite primly, she explained that they both worked and seldom had time with their children. As a result, they had made a vow to spend every minute of every weekend with them, because that was the right thing to do.

Then she told me how she felt about this decision. "You know what? I absolutely hate it."

There is no such thing as too much *quality* time alone with your children, but there is such a thing as too much *time* alone with your children.

This kind of begrudging togetherness will make monsters of the whole family. (You're at the end of your rope. And the kids can tell.) It also denies the parents the human privilege of socializing with their peers.

When people of the same age and stage of life get together to talk, invariably there'll be a discussion about the issues and mysteries of life at this moment in time. This is a necessary human ceremony. Four-year-olds do it. Teenagers do it. And we get to do it too.

Where do pacifiers go when babies lose them?

Why is it that when kids are crying because you're leaving them with a sitter, and you walk out the door and shut it, and you pause there for a minute with your ear on the door, you discover that the crying stops immediately?

Why do men have to hold the remote control?

One set of parents can be all tied up in knots about this stuff, while the others can laugh, sympathize, and help out.

It does worlds of good, too, to hang out with child-free people, to keep you from being a baby bore, and with older people who've been through it all and have moved on to another stage.

Socializing has a way of both cementing friendships and readjusting your world view. The working parents of young children, forever treadmilling in their hectic dual world, seeing life in tunnel vision, need that kind of glimpse of the global picture more than anybody.

To be perfectly, brutally honest, those of us who are still carrying diaper bags everywhere we go are not at our most scintillating time of life.

But we need to remember that at one time in our lives, we all had senses of humor and knew things that were going on in the world. And if we just keep our social networks open, there will be people ready to listen when we once again have intelligent things to say.

♦ QUALITY VACATIONS

They chanted, over and over, "Are we there yet?" They fought. They cried. They got lost. They got sunburned. They ate nothing but Snickers bars and went on a sugar rampage. They sobbed instead of napping. They played Game Boy in the back seat instead of looking out the window at the fabulous scenery. They got sick the night you had hard-to-get, reserved-three-months-in-advance tickets to the Hoop-Dee-Doo Revue.

They are children on vacation. They make mincemeat of us all.

How to Take a Family Vacation Without Feeling Like You Need a REAL Vacation Afterward

1. Lower your expectations.

Remember, this isn't your carefree student trip hitchhiking through France. It isn't your honeymoon. With children along, there is no way you can "vacate" from the greatest responsibility of your everyday life.

But a family vacation *is* a way you can enjoy, get to know, and learn to live with your nearest and dearest in a different environment, where the usual pressures are lifted.

2. Let there be space in your togetherness.

Mothers who do not work outside the home are better at this than those of us who do. They understand that you cannot interact with a child 18 hours a day and still maintain any semblance of a sane adult life. They go out alone, they talk to friends on the phone, they plant the kids in front of the television when necessary, and they have some time to themselves.

We working mothers tend to go at it full tilt on vacation, overplanning, overprotecting, overdoing it in general, and ending up overtired with overstimulated children.

Even though this is not a vacation from all your responsibilities, you can at least have some adult fun. You can share a rented house or condo with another family or with grandparents, so that the grown-ups can take turns baby-sitting and also have adult times together. You can drop the kids off with grandparents or a favorite aunt and uncle for a few days of the vacation, so you can spend some time doing strictly grown-up things.

Or you can choose a resort or vacation situation where child care or separate activities for kids are available. You can be playing tennis while they're out catching frogs.

Resorts, country inns, and bed-and-breakfasts can be terrific for kids. If children are allowed, there's more to explore than in the average motel.

At a small inn, sleeping babies and older kids can stay in the bedroom while Mom and Dad have a romantic dinner downstairs, just as much within reach as they would be at home. Not all inns welcome children, but a surprising number are happy to take them in.

Finally, if the children's father is a novice at solo child care, a vacation is an excellent time to give him a few hours on his own with the kids. Gives you a few hours off, too.

3. Be ready with a boredom bag.

A boredom bag is a bag full of age-appropriate books, activities, and electronics that is indispensable on a trip. What makes a boredom bag really work is just one thing: everything in it has to be absolutely brand new and never before seen. Contents must be kept a state secret until the trip actually begins.

A well-packed boredom bag can preclude at least three choruses of "Are we there yet?"

4. Don't buy food they won't eat.

Kids, by and large, are differently abled eaters. They can eat breakfast and lunch just about anywhere in the world, but you do yourself no favors by taking them out for a fancy dinner. You will either end up paying big money for food that goes untouched or, worse, your child may develop a craving for lobster.

Most nights, you'll depend on simple family restaurants. But once or twice a trip, kids are happy, as dinnertime looms, to be fed separately on a carry-out pizza or a grocery-bag picnic of healthy snacks. Then get a sitter and go out to dinner by yourselves.

5. Stand back when you visit grandparents.

While family visits are not strictly vacations—since your time is not really your own—they do crop up on the vacation schedule.

If your children don't get to see their grandparents often, show them pictures en route and tell them something about their grandparents' past and current lives.

Kids and grandparents have a right to form their own relationship with each other without hearing any old issues of yours. Children have an instinctive yearning for roots and love to hear about the people they came from.

Maybe you've heard the stories hundreds of times, but when you bring your children to visit your parents, stand back. Grandparents and grandchildren have their own ways of getting to know each other. They hold a special appreciation for each other, unweighted by any mixed feelings you may have. Parents are out of the loop.

6. Let them plan their own vacation.

Sooner or later, usually in the mid-teens, the kids are going to get to an age where they whine that your idea of a vacation—or in fact, going anywhere with you—is a dorky thing to do. Then it's time to let them take over. Give them a budget, a time limit, and a set of suggestions. Let them brainstorm with you. When you hit on a mutually agreeable place, let them borrow guidebooks from the library and plan out the itinerary.

7. Keep a journal.

At the end of each day, sit down with your child and help him remember and record what he did, what he learned, what surprised him, what he'd like to know more about. It won't mean much that night, but at the end of ten years it will be a very special souvenir.

And they can't ever say you didn't take them anywhere.

PARTING THOUGHT: MAKE IT REAL QUALITY TIME

In quality time, be it with an individual or with a group, it is the intensity of the attention, the understanding, the quality of the conversation, and the laughter that count, not the banality of the chore or the glamour of the adventure.

CHAPTER THREE

Is There Love After Parenthood?

"On our fifth wedding anniversary," a friend told me, "we hired two young single girls to babysit our toddlers while we went away for the weekend to celebrate. As we got into the car and waved good-bye, they broke into a chorus of 'Here Comes the Bride.'

"I had to laugh. They thought this weekend was all about sex. We knew it was all about sleep."

Besides the new rarity of sex and sleep, the single greatest danger to marriage after parenthood is the sheer lack of conversation.

I mean intimate conversation, where you get to know all the extraneous characters in each other's life, the trials, challenges, and joys of each day, where you get to reveal your dreams and heartaches and even have the leisure to keep track of each other's allergy symptoms on an ongoing basis.

Children change this for every marriage, but when both partners are working, there is twice as much chance that one of you will not be available for talk.

As new working parents, we all go from being couples who finish each other's sentences to being people who never even heard the first half of the sentence.

As time goes on, it only gets worse. To illustrate, here is an actual unexpurgated scene from my life:

The Setting: A small suburban kitchen

The Time: Last night, 8:30 p.m.

The Characters: DAD, MOM, son ALEC (age 11), the AU PAIR, son TED (age 14)

As the scene opens, I have just arrived home late from work and my husband and I have been sitting at the kitchen table talking for five minutes.

DAD: So then he said to me, "We might be paring down your department."

MOM: No! Did he really?

ALEC (*entering the room*): Mom, I'm trying to fix this guitar string and I can't.

DAD: Let me try.

AU PAIR (*entering*): I met the cutest guy at the beach. Do you want me to get some food tomorrow? Can I have a check for the groceries?

DAD: Okay, tomorrow I want you to bring this guitar back to the music store again and make them fix it.

ALEC: I'll stand there until they fix it.

MOM: Wait. I'll give you a check for the groceries. Remember we're all going away this weekend, so we won't need a lot of food.

AU PAIR: Right!

TED (*entering*): Mom, I recharged the battery on your computer. I think it ought to be okay now. Have you ever thought about putting a fax modem on it so you can message us from work?

MOM: A what?

ALEC *(sitting down with guitar)*: I've been working on some jazz improvisations. Wanna hear 'em? *(Begins to play.)*

DAD *(sighs, stands up)*: Okay, I guess we'd better clear these dishes.

AU PAIR: May I take the car? I promised Michelle I'd take her to the mall.

MOM: Ted! Don't tease the dog! I think he needs to go out.

ALEC *(singing)*: "Got those Bay City blues. . . . "

DAD: I don't know about the rest of you, but I'm going upstairs to read.

AU PAIR: I need to get some stuff for the camping trip this weekend.

TED: I think we could find a fax modem for about $150.

MOM: Alec, that's great! *(writing the check for the groceries)* A fax what? And so forth.

Clearly, what began as a kind of important conversation went up in smoke. Dad eventually quit; Mom stayed behind to write checks and give out permissions and assignments for the next day. Things were accomplished, but a conversation between Mom and Dad was not one of them.

Here's a conversation that actually fared a bit better:

MOM: The boiler man says we've got to clean out the chimney.

DAD: How much is that going to cost?

MOM: I have no idea. Gosh, I've got to get the kids in for checkups.

DAD: Okay, you do that, I'll do the boiler.

MOM: Tomorrow's the fifth grade concert. I'm taking half a day off to go.

DAD: I can't get away tomorrow. Should I feel guilty about this?

MOM: I bet there won't be a lot of fathers there. Do you have the money to pay for this American Express bill?

DAD: Next paycheck, probably.

Here, we pretty much completed the conversation, but it didn't do beans for our relationship. The almost unbearable tedium of this kind of conversation would be enough to strain a marriage all by itself.

Unfortunately, it's the only kind of conversation many of us can complete.

My husband and I have started having actual business meetings—scheduled, say, for 9:00 on a Saturday morning—when there's more than one matter to discuss. That way, we're sure to get the business done. But we don't make it a substitute for real conversation.

◆ HOW DO I LOVE THEE? JUST LOOK AT THIS TO-DO LIST!

What takes a while to learn, as one assumes the working parent life, is that the performance of household services does not prove a love relationship.

In *Fiddler on the Roof,* Tevye and Golda actually sing a song about this. He asks, "Do you love me?" And she responds, "For 25 years I've washed your clothes, cooked your meals, cleaned your house, given you children, milked the cow. . . . If that's not love, what is?"

But he is dissatisfied with this and answers, "Yes, but do you *love* me?"

It's easy to assume that because we are slaving away to keep the household together, the laundry and groceries organized, and the children safe and healthy, and because these things leave us exhausted and spent, these services are an adequate way of showing love to our life partner. They really are not.

We all know men who are so busy working and providing for the families they love that they haven't really talked to their wives in years.

The working mother version of this is being so busy on weekends and evenings coping with household maintenance, entertaining the children, and ferrying them one place and another that she's too tired and overwhelmed to relate to her man.

Does this show love? No. What it shows is that one has a need and a capability to keep everything clean and organized.

If whatever you are doing to keep your household under control is the same routine you'd be doing if there were no man in the house, then you're doing it for yourself, not for him.

The average husband would feel more loved if you dropped the vacuum cleaner and fell into his arms. Same way you'd feel if he suddenly cut the throttle on the lawn mower, grabbed you by the hand, and took you off for a walk in the woods.

Maybe you don't need to go grocery shopping tonight after all. Maybe you need to take your man out to dinner.

◆ THE WORKING MOTHER'S MOST INTIMATE LAMENT: TOO TIRED FOR LOVE

Why does the old marital spark sometimes burn so dim at this stage of life?

Maybe it's because the job provides an ongoing series of challenges and problems, with immediate victories and failures. There are always fires to be put out, achievable goals to see and meet.

The children, too, change every day and need constant attention to thrive and grow and learn. You can quickly feed their hunger, quell their tantrums, get them through the impossible part of their homework, and feel good about it right away.

But it is the very nature of marriage that it can be taken for granted a little.

The whole point of monogamy among thinking animals is to commit yourself to each other so that you can get on with a more productive life with shared commitments, and you don't have to go on flirting and mating and dating, feeling faint with love and flushed with romance, flying about on winged heels of passionate ecstasy, and never getting anything else done.

The marriage ceremony says: We are a unit now. On this solid rock, we'll build a new family and carry out the rest of our lives.

Somewhere in the marriage ceremony, too, the minister, rabbi, or judge always tells you that marriage takes work. This is like a fine-print clause that they must teach in marriage ceremony school: *Don't ever marry anybody without warning them about the hard part.*

Unfortunately, what with everybody weeping joyously and cooing over the bride's dress, nobody pays attention to this idea when it's being said. But years later, when you become a working parent, you find that the last thing you want to do is any more work. And certainly you don't want to work on this marriage business, the one part of your life you ought to trust to be stable day after day. The job and the kids are such a struggle, you feel, that you ought to be able to just relax and coast with this relationship.

Now, it would be very handy if our human needs for love and attention froze up from the day the first baby is born until the day the last one goes to college.

But it doesn't happen that way. We are all massive bundles of quivering insecure neurons and protons, and we all still need that one friend to talk to on a daily basis. We need help making life decisions, we need somebody with a shared history to laugh and cry with, and we need hugging.

The good news is that having children teaches us more about our own needs. If you have a husband in the house, and if you have children who resemble him, you can clearly see your husband's ways in the children—their version of ingratiating himself, of stomping his little foot, of whining for attention, and of wanting a big kiss good night. We disguise our needs in a more socially acceptable way, but those needs are much the same.

◆ HEY, BIG GUY! HOW ABOUT A DATE?

Real romance takes mystery, spontaneity, and leisure. These are the first three things to go when a couple attempts the strange stressed lifestyle of working parenthood. You get back parts of the three in the retirement years. In the meantime, you're just going to have to plan.

Back before you thought up this odd notion that it might be fun to live with a man, you and your main squeeze had to make plans to see each other. Is Tuesday good? How about Saturday? This was called dating.

The working parent lifestyle demands that you start prearranging your dates again. You must set a time to be together, and you must make sure that you are together *alone*.

There are ways to have dinner alone together in your own home. For example, if you do not plant the baby in her infant seat in the middle of the table as though she were an odd sort of centerpiece, you will have a better conversation. If you do not try to feed a child in a high chair during your own romantic meal *a deux* ("Open up! Here comes the airplane! Zooooom!"), an exchange of meaningful information and possible endearments is far more likely.

You may have to have a symbolic geographic location that says *We are alone here now; no children need tune in.* Maybe you can bribe the kids with a quarter apiece to watch cartoons every Saturday morning while you two eat breakfast in bed. Or, on a Friday night, feed the kids first and then set them up with a video and dessert in the den while you dine with candles and flowers in the dining room.

Maybe your retreat will be the back stoop, the front porch, the dining room table, the two wing chairs in front of the fire.

But it can be awfully hard to fence a child out in his own home. That's why there's nothing like getting out of the house.

WE'RE OUTTA HERE!

Many of us feel that because we spend so much time working outside the home—away from our adorable cuddly darlings in their footie pajamas, away from our own warm kitchen and that dishwasher that always needs unloading and the laundry that always needs folding—we ought to always be there when we're not working, whether we feel like it or not.

Try to get over this.

You do your children no favors by letting them think that they are the very center of your life, even if it's true. As a friend of mine likes to say, "My mother *lived* for me. I wish she hadn't."

If you still feel guilty, remember that the preservation of your marriage is absolutely key to their happiness and sanity. Whether it's a trip to Europe or a walk around the neighborhood, get out of the house. Together. Alone.

BURGER, FRIES, NO KIDS, NO DISHES

Through rain, through snow, through pockets of poverty and eras of overload, arrange to have a dinner date out once a week, no matter what. The experience forces the two of you to sit there, face to face, for at least one entire hour, with nobody jumping up for more food or to clear the table.

If you can, go someplace where children are barred. If you've given your own children the slip for the evening, you certainly don't want somebody else's running up and down the aisles.

It's funny how your choice of restaurant can change after you have children. Suddenly, the quality of the food doesn't matter so much anymore. All you really want are atmosphere, service, and relative silence.

But you can do without that if you have to. Once, during a time of what I'll call problematic cash flow, my husband resisted our weekly dinner date on financial grounds. I promised him I'd design a mystery date that would cost under $10. We ended up at the local fast-food joint. Had a good time, too.

Whether your dinner date is at the Ritz-Carlton or on a blanket at the local park, set aside the time in advance, as you did in your dating years. If the time comes and you don't feel like it, go anyway.

BEING THERE

Once you spirit your man away from his darling children, his beloved remote control, and his La-Z-Boy, try not to fritter away this precious time in

◆ DARLING, I FEEL A LITTLE HOSTILE ◆

Realistically, you must be prepared to fight during a date. Since the average couple fights once a month, and given that your weekly dinner is your only opportunity for private conversation, chances are one in four that the conversation will get a little heated. Try not to be freaked out by this normal development.

But, as a courtesy to your mate, it's a good idea not to have a violent argument anywhere that the bill totals over $30.

---

idle chit-chat. You may even declare a moratorium on the subject of the children and home repair and skip right to the news of the world and the news of his life.

As you do this, try to spend as much time listening as you do talking.

Your attention is widely divided at this point in your life. You no longer have the time and emotional energy that was once his alone, the time to sense his inner turmoil or get every detail of his every day. Your intuition is fragmented, so he must tell you what's happening. Let him do it.

And he ought to do the same for you.

Your personal conversations before children were like daily newspapers, long and detailed and hardly digested. Now they must be like weekly newsmagazines, the stories shorter, with fewer details, but deeper and told with the benefit of hindsight and some accrued wisdom. They ought to be much more interesting now.

◆ QUALITY TIME, COUPLES ONLY

The once-a-week dinner is the bare minimum requirement for keeping a relationship alive. But there are other ways for the two of you to spend time together.

Go away for the weekend together once in a while. You'll know this is overdue if you get lost on the way out of town because you're so busy talking to each other. Ideally, working parents should go away for the weekend once a quarter.

But I don't know anybody who can manage this. Instead, you ought to just isolate some of the activities you would do if you were going away together for the weekend and practice one at a time.

For example, grocery shopping, which is deadly dull as a solo activity, can make a fun date. Food is sensuous, after all, and picking out food can make a remarkably warm and bonding activity.

Then there is clothes shopping. The trouble with clothes shopping with husbands is that they have the attention span of hummingbirds and do not understand the activity of cruising the racks, considering the colors, feeling the goods. They do not understand shopping as spectator sport with no preordained goal in view.

Men only go shopping if they need boxer shorts or a suit. They don't get the idea of attending a big sale simply to reassure yourself that there is nothing there that you can't live without.

But the upside of going clothes shopping with a man, especially if you're going because you need to buy something, is that he will tell you right away if that outfit makes you look more like Julia Roberts or Queen Elizabeth.

He will not cock his head, squint, think it over, hike up the hem, unbutton the top button, read the price tag, or try to visualize it with the right shoes. He will just briefly look up and say, "Naah" or "Yesss!"

If he likes it well enough, he might buy it for you.

If your man can go clothes shopping with you, you can probably go electronics shopping with him. Then there's mall walking, woods hiking, ballroom dancing lessons, bike riding, or just plain joyriding.

When It Seems Impossible

There will be entire years in your life when it will seem impossible for the two of you to get out the front door together. For example:

1. When you have a baby who gets one ear infection after another.
2. When you have three toddlers under the age of six.
3. When your son takes up hockey seriously.

But please remember:

1. You cannot cure a sick child by staying home with him 24 hours a day. Twenty hours is plenty.

2. Kids enjoy having a different referee now and then.

3. Your children's athletic schedule is not a substitute for your personal, social, or love life.

Yes, it may seem impossible, but keep trying.

LOVE AND THE COMMUNICATIONS REVOLUTION

How else can you communicate with a man you rarely get to see? Let us count the ways.

1. Telephone

2. Answering machine

3. Cellular phone

4. Beeper

5. Fax

6. E-mail

7. U.S. Mail

8. FedEx

9. Messenger

10. Flowers by wire (The best thing about sending a man flowers at the office is that he has to spend the whole day explaining who they come from. And he loves every minute of it.)

PARTING THOUGHT: GIVE YOUR LOVE LIFE PRIORITY

However you reach out and touch your man, remember that you both still have a right to an adult love life.

Working on your relationship to keep it alive and well is one of the best things you can do for yourself—and for your children.

In Loco Parentis

Coping with Nanny Panic and Day-Care Dilemmas

Every one of us secretly, secretly, secretly wishes that we could go without child care. In fact, every single time I need to change child-care arrangements, I actually consider quitting work.

I sit down with a piece of paper and figure out what I'd save on pantyhose, commuting cost, and coffee shop tuna fish sandwiches versus the cut in income. Then I calculate my chances of rejoining the workforce as a blue-haired arthritic lady on a walker the year my last child goes to college. Of course, the numbers never work out, so I sigh and go back to work.

Why is it that perfectly capable women who can win the Nobel prize, save lives, and run their own businesses suddenly find themselves paralyzed at the thought of finding child care?

Well, look. Your children are your greatest treasures. And at the time you begin your quest, all potential child-care providers are total strangers.

Often, we expect too much. We want someone like ourselves—bright, witty, responsible, loving, imaginative, patient, well-mannered, and cheerful. Also, we want her to be smart, but not so smart that she's going to get bored in two months and leave us to go to medical school.

And the risk is terrific. You could actually marry and divorce a guy with less personal risk than that involved in placing your child in a faulty child-care situation. We've all heard those Nanny Dearest stories and the Day Care Center from Hell stories and we all shove them to the back of our minds . . . *until that moment when we are looking for child care again.*

This sort of fear is tantamount to being afraid to drive a car because car crashes happen. In fact, for every car crash there are millions of safely completed drives per day. And for every bad nanny and dreadful child-care center, there are millions more that are good.

So even though all these out-of-whack hopes and fears are real and natural and occur to every one of us hunting for child care, we must put them all aside.

◆ DREAM ON DEPARTMENT

In an ideal world, we would all bring our children to our place of employment and walk them into a fabulous day-care center stuffed with stimulating, colorful, educational toys. The center would be staffed by caring, cheerful nurses and teachers with doctorates in first aid, child development, and primary education. And we could visit them whenever we wanted to during the day and pick them up after work, no matter what time that was.

If you are fortunate enough to work in one of the very small percentage of American workplaces that have taken this step to avoid the trained-female brain drain, then you are fortunate indeed.

Otherwise, you have these options: a day-care center, family day care, or a caregiver in your home.

◆ A DAY CARE CENTER

Typical cost: $55 to $200 per week per child.

Good group day care is hard to find. I once knew a professional woman who researched her whole city for the best day-care center and then moved close to it. Then she conceived the child. Then she signed the child up on the waiting list. Then the child was born. And nobody thought she was crazy.

Pros: There are a lot of children around to play with. There can be wide-open spaces and child-size furniture, along with a wider variety of toys and learning situations than children would have anywhere else.

Kids in day care learn both sharing and independence. Children without siblings can especially benefit from hanging out with a bunch of other kids all day.

Cons: The day-care center door usually slams shut promptly at a certain hour, and getting there on time can put you in a race against the clock that can start early in the day. In the end, when you have to rush out of work in mid-thought and rescue your child from what you now perceive as the vicious, inflexible grip of your day-care center, you are not having good feelings about it anymore.

How to Kick the Tires on a Day-Care Center

1. Visit the center and ask questions about adult-child ratio, flexible schedules, staff turnover, play space, toys, furniture, and other facilities. Look at outdoor space, safety precautions, the children's general welfare. Get references from other parents, too.

2. On your whole checklist, the most important thing for your child is consistent care—that he sees the same caregivers there month after month or at least sees enough of the same people to feel safe. The director will tell you the usual details, but go to staffers as well to ask about turnover and quality of life for workers. How many people have left lately? What are their benefits and vacations like? Is the work satisfying? What is the general employee happiness level?

3. Even more important than anything on the checklist, says a veteran child-care provider, is sheer gut instinct. How you feel when you're in the day-care center, if it makes you comfortable, if you like the noise level and the structure level, and if you think you can communicate with these people and trust them with your children—all these are more important than any number of educational toys.

WHAT YOU DON'T WANT TO SEE
WHEN YOU VISIT A DAY-CARE CENTER

1. Kids are crying and nobody's paying attention.

2. Kids are fighting and nobody's stopping them.

3. Kids are lined up, sitting in time-out chairs.

4. Kids are wandering around bored and glassy-eyed.

5. Day-care providers are reading the want ads.

6. Day-care providers are wearing a lot of black leather and listening to heavy metal music.

7. Staffers are discussing their love lives, last night's episode of "Married with Children," or the sweater sale at Marshall's, chatting mostly with each other instead of interacting with the kids.

Therefore: Good day care will work well for you as long as you find the right center, you have good backup for emergency sick days, and either you or your husband is absolutely certain of being able to leave work at the same time every day.

Hint: During the first few days of day care, your child may experience separation anxiety. Or you might. Most staffers will let you sit and watch and weep as long as you need to before you go to work. But leave when your day-care center director boots you out. Your child can be confused by your ongoing presence if you stay too long.

What really can hurt is when you pick them up at the end of the day and they don't want to go home. Relax. This is a very positive sign.

◆ FAMILY DAY CARE

Typical cost: $60 to $150 per week per child.

Family day care—leaving your child in another woman's home for the day—is by far the most common kind of paid child-care arrangement.

Pros: Family day care can be very reasonably priced. Providers are often women who love children and child care and who have children of their own. Because groups are smaller than in group day care, your child will get more attention. Studies have shown that family day-care providers can be better trained and more professional than day-care providers in your own home.

Cons: Because family day care may be informal and unlicensed, it bears a little more investigation up front. Also, more often than in center day care, some family day-care mothers aren't really into other people's kids. They're just doing it as a default job so they can stay home with their own kids. Or they may be doing it just for the money.

WHAT TO LOOK FOR IN FAMILY DAY CARE

1. Is there room for the kids to run around, both indoors and out?
2. Are there enough toys and books? Or will there be fights over sharing?
3. Do manners have a part in the "curriculum"?
4. Are there house rules? What are they?

5. What are the house mother's own kids like?

6. Does she get good personal references (from neighbors or church and community folk) as well as professional references?

7. Are there assistants? Who are they? What is the child/helper ratio?

8. And what happens when the day-care provider herself is sick? Usually, the burden of finding a replacement is on her, not on you. But either way, find out in advance.

How to Tell That There Might Be Something Fishy about Your Family Day Care

- Your child often comes home hungry.
- Your child is oddly familiar with the plot line of "General Hospital."
- Your child imitates Mrs. Smith's snoring during her nap.
- Your child has learned how to play Mortal Kombat somewhere.
- Your child won't sleep at night because she says she's been sleeping all day.

- You can't get through to the family day-care home during the day because the line is always busy.
- Your child talks about various "uncles" who drop by regularly.
- Your four-year-old proudly announces she was "in charge" for a while today while Mrs. Smith ran out to do an errand.

WARNING: BLOOD IS ICKIER THAN WATER

The one kind of day care that is consistently tricky is care by a relative. With grandmothers there are issues of how you're bringing the child up. He may experience one kind of spoiling at grandma's, another at your house.

And there may be the question of how much *care* is going into the child care. Is an aunt or grandmother caring for your child primarily because it's easy, inexpensive (or free), and convenient for you?

Any time you are paying a relative for anything, you are in danger of destroying the relationship. Anytime you are not paying for child care, you have no control over the quality of your child's care or your caregiver's commitment and hours.

◆ THE CARE AND FEEDING OF
A GOOD DAY-CARE PROVIDER

Whether you are using center care or family care, your day-care providers are the heart and soul of your child's experience.

Center providers make an average of $12,000 a year, while family day-care providers make $10,000 a year on average. It's not much for the hours, the stress, the patience, the loyalty, the fidelity, and the kindness.

If you have found somebody you trust with your children, let her know that you respect her as well. This is more than nice; it is necessary.

• Be on time with drop-off and pick-up. If you can't, call in advance to say so. She has a schedule, too.

• Trust your day-care provider and let her know it. Shower her with support and genuine compliments. Ask how her day went, as well as how your child's day went. Get to know her personally: what her family situation is like, what pressures she's under, what her goals and interests are. Ask about these things as you would with a friend.

• Bring surprise presents for her or for the group now and then: some fruit, some pastry, a book to share, a bunch of flowers.

• If you feel you have a criticism and you're afraid to speak up, phrase it as a question instead. Why are Alec's shirts always wet at the end of the day? (He refuses to put on his plastic smock at the water table.) Why are the remains of Ted's lunch still in his lunch box all smelly and yucky at day's end? (The day-care provider wanted to let you know what he didn't eat.)

Taking care of six or nine or twelve kids involves a whole different set of rules than caring for one or two. So day-care providers prefer that you ask before you criticize, and that you give them a chance to explain the procedures and rituals of the center.

- Volunteer to give a few hours' help at the center, organize a field trip, or bring in a special activity or guest speaker.

- When you can, pitch in at day's end with furniture rearrangement, clean-up, and general helpfulness that signals your sentiment, "I know this is a hard job. Let me help."

- Promote center-parent school spirit by starting a parents' newsletter, tossing a party for parents and caregivers, and generally showing your willingness to participate and your respect for the caregivers' work.

- Remember your caregiver on her birthday, at Christmas, and at the end of your term together. A good caregiver is a kind of saint. Nothing can really pay for the affection, stimulation, and patience she is giving your children. Be very kind.

- Every once in a while, say, "I don't know *how* you do it!" Because, you know, you really don't.

♦ A CAREGIVER IN YOUR HOME

If you have more than two children, or if your hours are irregular, a caregiver in your home is worth considering. Home caregivers have all sorts of titles and job designations. Here are some of the accepted terms and what they mean.

A HOUSEKEEPER

Cost: $250 and up per week.

Pros: A housekeeper tends your children but also cleans the house and cooks. The ideal housekeeper drives so that she can pick up groceries and do errands. She also speaks English, because even if your kids are too young to talk, she may have to talk to a repairman, a doctor, or some other child's mother. A good housekeeper helps keep you and your house organized.

Cons: Housekeepers cost the earth.

Sometimes, they are more interested in keeping house than keeping children. Some will vacuum like demons while your kids sit and watch.

Naturally, with older children this could be no problem at all. They should be doing their homework anyway.

    Hint: If you find a housekeeper who seems gifted in both cleaning and child care, hire her and double her salary immediately.

A NANNY

    Typical cost: $200 and up per week.

    Nannies could be young graduates of the growing number of nanny schools here and abroad. Or they could simply be experienced women who have chosen to make a lifelong career of child care.

    Pros: Nannies are sticklers for manners, field trips, and mind-expanding activities. They are ideal for upscale kids whose parents travel a lot, and they may stay with the family for years. Perhaps better trained for the job than you are, they may share child-raising advice with you.

    Cons: On the other hand, they may share child-raising advice with you. Also, cleaning *anything* is officially not part of the job description. I once heard of a nanny who refused to mop up a splash of orange juice from her toddler-charge's snack because she didn't consider it part of her child-care job.

Therefore: If you can afford a nanny, get one—as long as you can afford a butler, too.

Hint: If you go this route, clarify your mutual expectations about dishes, toy clean-up, laundry, and so on in advance.

A Babysitter

Cost: $3 to $15 an hour. More for daytime sitters than for nighttime sitters.

Pros: So maybe she didn't go to nanny school. A loving, experienced sitter is generally high on common sense. She may have raised children of her own or have recently been a child herself, and she may be more willing to pitch in with light housework, especially the laundry, kitchen mess, and toy spills that children generate. Regardless of age, people who call themselves babysitters are not likely to tell you how to bring up your children.

Cons: A babysitter may not stay with you long. Young babysitters are generally on their way to another career, while older ones may be on the brink of retirement.

Hint: When hiring teenage babysitters for evenings out, look for girls and boys who are in it for the money or out of genuine interest and not just for something to do. If they say they have to ask their parents and never call you back, it means they're waiting for a better invitation. Put these on the bottom of your list, and call them in times of desperation only. Your own personal plans should never be at the mercy of a teenage babysitter. You deserve the evening out more than she does.

An Au Pair

Typical cost: About $230 a week, including agency fee.

A foreign au pair (which means, literally, "on equal terms with the family") is young (17 to 26 years old) and lives with your family, usually for a year, with an educational visa, if she's in this country legally.

Pros: An au pair can be the most inexpensive way to go for live-in child care.

She takes a big-sister position in the family and can provide you with another young woman to chat with. She brings her culture and language into your home (along with a whole lot of rock music) and shares them with the children, enlarging their world. She is young enough to be a buddy to the kids, but old enough to maintain discipline.

Because she lives in, an au pair provides you with maximum flexibility concerning hours, even if you travel in your job. She will also come along on family trips if you like and help with the children while you play.

She can become a family friend for life, and, if you plan carefully, you can eventually end up with a different family to visit in every country in Europe.

Cons: Because she's sort of a semi-guest, you will have to sacrifice some of your family privacy. Naturally you owe your au pair some warm welcoming events and orientation in the first few weeks. But as time goes on, she will learn to rely on her growing list of same-age friends for both entertainment and soul-baring.

In the beginning, you may have to cope with her homesickness. And throughout your time together, you may find yourself mothering her and dealing with her emotional issues.

Au pairs can be inexperienced drivers, and fender benders are common. Through some miracle, for which I have no provable figures and which is not based on any scientific fact, children are rarely in the car when these minor accidents happen. Must be that there *is* a God.

Therefore: An au pair gives you maximum value by the hour, lacking only age and experience. Au pairs are best for mothers who work from home or close to home or for families with older kids. Another consideration is how many other au pairs are stationed in your area. In rural areas, au pairs miss peer social life more than they miss their mothers.

Hint: It's well worth it to use a legal, reputable au pair agency to find your au pair, rather than going it alone. You may not go to jail for importing an au pair illegally, but you may suddenly find that your child care has been hastily deported.

Au pair agencies will handle the flights, legalities, visas, orientation, and counseling for your au pair. Agencies also introduce local au pairs to each other so they can have buddies for all-important peer socializing and travel. And if one au pair doesn't work out in the first few weeks, they'll send you a different one.

Hint: Try to avoid hiring the children of your foreign friends and relatives for an au pair job. Girls who come through friends often think they're going to have a wonderful guest-like experience, when what you need is solid help. Somewhere in the gap, there's a good chance you'll muck up the friendship.

◆ HOW TO HIRE A HOUSEKEEPER, BABYSITTER, OR IN-HOME CAREGIVER

1. First of all, remember that you are General Patton. This is war, and you are in charge. This process may very well take a month or more. You'd spend at least that much time car shopping, wouldn't you?

2. Make a list of duties you would like your caregiver to perform for you. This will vary according to your interests, your work schedule, the ages and stages of your children, and so forth. Figure out if what you really want and really need is a housekeeper, a nanny, a babysitter, or an au pair (see previous descriptions).

3. Then ask your fellow neighborhood working moms or a local employment agency what the going rates are for each in your town and see if you can afford it.

4. Adjust your expectations according to your budget. Sometimes an in-home caregiver is cheaper than keeping two children in day care.

5. Decide if you want live-in or live-out.

Live-in gives you greater flexibility with your work hours and play hours, if you need that. But if your live-in caregiver does not have her own family and friends nearby, you are taking on some responsibility for her private life. You also sacrifice some privacy.

Live-out help gives you much more privacy but often less flexibility. If your sitter has children of her own, she may have to streak out every night at six, which limits your freedom. Also, live-out caregivers may have to support whole other households and understandably need a hefty salary to do so. If your caregiver does not have her own transportation, you may have to drive her to and from your home.

6. Now that you have the job description, line up the candidates. Look in your local paper, call local agencies (check their fees and guarantees, always), talk to everybody you know, and place ads in your church, your school, your Y, your employee newsletter.

Place an ad in your local paper if you wish, but don't be surprised if you hear from a lot of people who don't fit your requirements at all. Many job seekers are hoping you were just kidding about needing someone who drives.

7. Check one reference before you invite anyone to your home for an interview.

Now for the interview!

8. After an initial chat, introduce the potential caregiver to your children, and let the kids hang out during part of the interview to see how she interacts with them and what vibes the kids pick up. Invent an excuse to leave them alone for a few minutes, and then spy on them.

9. Ask questions. Why is she in this line of work? What experience does she have? What is her own family configuration? How would she handle certain situations that might come up? Use real examples that have baffled you or a previous sitter. They might well recur.

10. Describe the job in as much detail as possible, even the grisly parts. If it's a hard job, let her know. If one child has a learning disability, a behavioral disorder, or special dietary needs, mention that up front. If your kids are impossibly messy and you expect her to clean up after them, let her know.

Throw into the description every possible chore and duty you want done. Later on, if it proves too much, it's easier to take away duties than to add them.

11. Let her ask questions. The first sitter I ever hired won the job with one question about my four-month-old: "Should I pick him up every time he cries?" Though not a mother herself, she'd chosen one of the key issues of baby care, one that determines a mothering style, and showed a desire to be consistent with it. She was one of the best sitters we ever had.

On the other hand, the dumbest interview question I ever heard was "Will I have to cut my long hair short?" This sitter's other good qualities made her worth the gamble, and she, too, turned into one of our best.

12. At the end of the interview, get the names of more references and say you'll call back as soon as you've checked them.

This is very important: Even if she has come through an agency, call all the references. Call the last person she worked for as well. Ask about her strengths and weaknesses. By collecting a variety of opinions, you'll come up with a good rounded picture of your candidate.

Even if you decide against her, let her know. She may be holding up her job search for you.

If she seems worth a try, give her a try. Once you find somebody who seems fantastic—or even good enough—ask her to babysit your kids for an afternoon or an evening. If that works, offer her a trial period on the job.

Ten Phrases You Don't Want to Hear from a Potential Caregiver

1. "I thought I'd do this as a year off before I go back to college." (A noble thought, but it's a job, not a year off.)

2. "I do smoke a little, but I wouldn't do it in the house or in front of the children." (So the kids are at each other's throats with kitchen knives while she's sneaking a quick one behind the garage.)

3. "I don't drive a stick shift." (You'll try to teach her, but you have visions of your car stalling, jolting, and shoving its way around town with your kids in the back seat.)

4. "I don't do . . . windows, laundry, cooking, playdates with other people's kids," etc. (It's honest and up front, but, even if you don't need any of those services, it may betray a certain attitude problem.)

5. "Yours is the kind of family I could really get attached to." (She'll have tea at the kitchen table with you when you get home from work; she'll pour out her troubles to you; she'll borrow money from you; she'll be there on Christmas day whether you invited her or not; she'll pout if you don't take her along on the family vacation.)

6. "My father got up and left when I was six, and it's been just us girls ever since." (This could be just fine. Or she could ignore or flirt with your husband or glom onto your family for dear life.)

7. "Is it okay if my boyfriend spends the night sometimes?" (Wouldn't it be nicer for everybody if she just went to his place?)

8. "Please, I really, really need this job." (Probably she's lost five or six in the last year.)

9. "Yes, missus, yes, missus, yes, missus." (She doesn't understand a word you're saying.)

10. "I just need an hour a week off to visit my probation officer." (Okay, maybe she deserves another chance. But not necessarily from you.)

I Said "Heat up the Bottle," Not "Heat up the Battle"

For many of us, a child's caregiver may be the first and perhaps only employee we ever have. The difficulty of "bossing" somebody who may be older than you are and admittedly more experienced with children is rarely expressed, and the task is often botched. Besides your own vague feeling of insecurity about being the boss, you may be dealing with somebody from a different culture, who may have a different first language.

Therefore, instructions to the sitter, whether written, oral, or both, must be clear and simple. If she makes mistakes, correct them with a reissuance or perhaps a rewording of the original request.

You may sound dumb, but only to yourself. With your caregiver, make yourself perfectly clear, no matter how stupid you sound.

This is your house, your children. The caregiver needs your guidance. Don't give up if she doesn't get it right the first time. All of us sometimes need coaching in a new and nervous-making situation. She's got to get used to your style, too.

On the other hand, two warnings on the same subject ought to be enough for such an important mission. If she twice hasn't heard you on issues discussed in advance, what kind of judgment will she use in an emergency?

◆ I DON'T THINK THIS IS WORKING OUT

One of life's truly bum moments is having to admit you've made a mistake. It is especially cutting, wounding, and hard to admit that you've made a child-care mistake. After all, this is your *most serious responsibility.* How could you blow it?

It's very easy—and we've all done this—to keep an inadequate child-care situation going too long because we can't admit we've been wrong or because there's been no clear firing offense.

In fact, child care is a gamble. You are asking someone to do an important job that you are not there to watch. It is an intimate situation that involves many subtleties and small details, and there are a million ways a person can go wrong.

Some of them are harmless. Some of them are scary. Any of them could take a long time to discover. If you find you've made a mistake, try not to beat yourself up.

But you mustn't be afraid to make a change, either. Yes, it's arduous to interview and retrain, but the alternatives—everything from mildly distracting guilt and anxiety at work to serious consequences too hideous to mention—are off the scale.

The nature of the firing offense will vary according to your own standards and expectations in child care. There is always an element of gambling and uncertainty that you must allow for—accidents can happen even when the child is in *your* care—but beyond that, a feeling of mistrust is quite enough.

Perhaps the caregiver is not sensible enough or sane enough. If you find yourself worrying past the point you would over any reasonable gamble, it's time to tell her it's not working.

If sanity is an issue, or theft, or willful acts of noncooperation with the house rules, it's best to ask the caregiver to leave immediately, without notice. You don't want a rejected, angry person left alone with your children.

Sometimes, though, sitters are fired for being too close to the children. That seems unfair. Closeness is not a firing offense. At certain preschool ages, children tend to cling to the person they just spent the most time with, and that could be the babysitter or the day-care provider. Be glad your child likes the caregiver—it means he's having a pleasurable and enriching experience all day.

The child always knows darned well which one is her mother, and, after she's had a few minutes of intense attention from you, she'll cling to you as well.

◆ TEN WAYS TO TELL YOUR CAREGIVER YOU LOVE HER

When you are entrusting your children to a caregiver, she deserves your utmost respect. It doesn't matter that she's not your best friend or best-friend material—that's not part of the job.

1. Here's the most important thing: let her know you trust her. If she's new and you're not sure, at least fake it. People who feel totally *trusted and in charge* always do their best.

2. Respect the fact that she's got a life, too. Let her know at the beginning of each week if she's needed for early mornings, late nights, or special errands and chores. Don't sign her up for extra duty without asking first. If there's a last-minute change, be apologetic.

3. Be generous! Your caregiver's trustworthiness and dedication to your children are things money cannot buy. Still, money makes a dandy reward. Pay extra for overtime, and give spot bonuses for extra-special assignments. Besides hard cash, be generous with your time, your ear, your advice, and whatever else you have to give.

4. If you're taking a day off and you can manage it, give her a day off with pay, too.

5. Use frequent praise when things are going right, and dole out new instructions when they're not. Everybody needs feedback, even the corrective kind. It shows she's being taken seriously.

6. If you take your nanny or au pair on vacation and expect her to work, give her free time to explore. But working vacations—your business trip to Omaha while breast feeding, your family reunion, your trip to the isolated family vacation cabin where she's trapped without even a television—do not substitute for real vacations.

Au pairs especially, with their one-year time frame, need to have their own vacation time to go to Orlando, Niagara Falls, the Grand Canyon, and Los Angeles (the top four au pair destinations) with their same-age friends, so they can stay up all night and howl.

7. Give her wheels—and yourself some freedom. The two best reasons to allow your au pair or nanny use of a car are a) so she won't hang around the house in her off hours and get in your way and b) so you won't have to drive her everywhere she wants to go.

The car shouldn't be too fancy, though, or she'll become the designated driver for her whole crowd and you will fret over every scratch. Loan her a car any teenager would be roundly ashamed of . . . but be sure it works well enough that she won't call you for a jump-start at midnight.

8. As with any caregiver, don't forget presents, compliments, and thanks. Birthdays and holidays can be especially hard for people far away from home, so do make a fuss about them. Perhaps the two of you could reproduce some home-country customs and recipes in your home so she'll feel more comfortable.

9. If you're thinking of making extra plans for your sitter, like having other children over for a playdate or loaning her services to another family, ask her first.

10. Side with your sitter when the kids are whining about her, at least until you hear both sides of the story. While everybody makes mistakes sometimes, don't let the kids think that they can control the situation or that she works for them. If necessary, discuss house rules with her privately, but reinforce her authority in front of the children.

PARTING THOUGHT:
YOUR CAREGIVER IS YOUR PARTNER

Since we must have substitute care for our children, we must also try for a noble and generous attitude about it. A good caregiver is your partner in the difficult job of helping your children grow—not your competition or your slave.

Jealousy should be the least of your worries. Well-adjusted children are capable of closeness with many adults at the same time—and that is how they were brought up in tribes and villages for centuries. The more people children can sense are truly caring about them, the better off they are.

CHAPTER FIVE

School and the Working Mother

The school arena is where you are most likely to come across the great divide in motherhood. I am speaking of Mothers Who Work Outside the Home and Mothers Who Work Within the Home.

Those are the politically correct titles for these two groups; no longer is it Working Mothers and Nonworking Mothers. The so-called nonworking mothers always disliked those designations because it implied they didn't work, when in fact they do Work Within the Home. A lot.

These newer titles, Mothers Who Work Outside the Home and Mothers Who Work Within the Home, make it clear that *both* groups work. I acknowledge this fact, and I'd like to add that in my life I have belonged to both groups and have equal respect for each. I'd like to ask permission from the PC Police to refer to the two groups hereafter as the Jobbed and the Jobless, just for brevity's sake.

Thank you.

Now, can we talk?

There is, in this culture at this time, a certain amount of tension between these two groups. That is because we suspect each other of certain subversive thoughts.

The Jobbed suspect the Jobless are thinking, "Those working women are terrible mothers, and they're just doing this to fulfill their stupid ambitions or because they're greedy for money and they think that's more important than their children. Can't they make do with less?"

The Jobless suspect the Jobbed are thinking, "Why on earth would any woman want to hang around the house all day wiping noses and scrubbing floors? They must be dunces. Why don't they get a life?"

Naturally, these perceptions, accurate or not, may create a certain underlying conflict, and it comes out most clearly at school. At every school I've ever known, the Jobless are the ones always assuming leadership positions in the PTA and fund-raising events and Teacher Appreciation Day.

Sometimes, we Jobbed mothers compete with the Jobless because we're just so used to being dutiful. Or perhaps we're trying to prove to ourselves and the world that, even though we work outside the home, we are still interested in the school and are therefore good mothers.

Having been, as I said, on both sides of this issue, my advice about PTA Power is this: Let the Jobless have it. It's fun, yes; it's a bonding thing; it's a way of making friends in the community. But it is not a territory for working moms. Being a big deal at the school is part of the Jobless mothers' role in life, and they will actually feel resentful if we try to step in and interfere.

However, you *are* expected to pitch in and do your part as a drone if not as a queen bee. Also, if you are in a position to do so, the more goodies you bring home from work that will in some way benefit the school, the more of a heroine you can be.

If, when asked to volunteer, you say, "No, I can't because I work," you give all of us a bad name, and we will all come find you and beat you.

When asked to volunteer, the correct thing to say is "I don't have a lot of time and don't have any real organizational talents. But I really want to help, and I could make a few phone calls/brownies/costumes."

Or "I can't help decorate on Friday for the school fair, but I'd be happy to staff a booth on Saturday and then stay afterward and pick up the garbage and sweep the floor."

Or "I can't work on the benefit auction catalog, but I could bring a whole slew of our new lipsticks home from work to auction off."

THREE RULES FOR WORKING MOMS VOLUNTEERING AT SCHOOL

1. Keep your volunteering to times and places you can manage: at home and on weekends. If you sign up for something that involves weekday meetings and then you can't show up, you'll get a reputation as a slacker.

2. Instead of the time you can't give, contribute things and services from your work, which will build goodwill both for your business and yourself.

Donate pies from your diner or free facials from your salon or three hours of tax help from your office, even if you have to buy them yourself at the employee rate.

3. Try to do the kind of volunteering that includes your children. Otherwise you'll be sitting in some meeting on a Tuesday night making posters with other moms wondering, *Why am I here when I want to be home with my children, whom I haven't seen all day?*

Doing volunteer work *with* your children makes for excellent quality time, and it sets a good example about community work. Run a booth at the fair with your kids. Set up, clean up, sell tickets, and count the proceeds with your bigger kids. Involving them teaches them the fun and beauty of volunteer work and gives them the joy of being with you.

And, of course, it is *their* school. By showing them your willingness to help out with their cause, they may well return the favor sometime and help out with some cause of yours.

◆ TEACHERS AND YOU

Most teachers are working mothers themselves, which is a wonderful boon. They are your allies and therefore will understand any problems you may have with getting school-related things done, from baking for a Wednesday bake sale to scheduling a parent-teacher conference for the hours before work.

Indeed, it was a teacher who was also a mother of five who gave me a terrific hint about helping my third-grader get his homework done. At the time, Ted's homework had become a part-time job for me, and it had also turned me into a temperamentally challenged person at that hour every day. By which I mean there was lots of screaming. So, this wise teacher said, "Hire a neighborhood teenager to come help him after school. It will help him concentrate, and you won't have to get involved."

I have nothing but the highest praise for the teachers of America, who have chosen to spend long, tedious days teaching our children the difference between 5 and s, between carnivores and herbivores, between synonyms and antonyms. All of this while keeping the kids seated and quiet. They should all get double pay.

But every once in awhile you will come across the rare teacher who is hostile to working mothers. This may be because:

1. She is childless but loves kids so much that she cannot imagine why someone lucky enough to have one would then go back to work, or

2. He sees that a child has problems in school and, unwilling to blame himself and unable to figure out what is wrong with the child, resorts to the next easiest target: the fact that the mother works, or

3. She has been in the job so long, feeling overworked and underpaid, that she hates all the parents anyway—and half the kids as well.

THE PARENT-TEACHER CONFERENCE

It was surely a teacher belonging to one of these rare lower forms who said to a working mother of my acquaintance, when she showed up for a conference, "Oh, so Jason *does* have a mother!"

The mother in question is the CEO of a large company and not thin-skinned, but the remark was painful enough to stay with her for quite a while. None of us likes to be judged on the quality of our motherhood.

But malevolent teachers have a special capability to hurt us. They know our children almost intimately, and we can be extremely sensitive to their criticism. Unlike our sisters, the Jobless mothers, we all carry just a scintilla of uncertainty about whether our children would be better off if we didn't work. So when things aren't perfect at school, we are very tempted to blame ourselves.

But hey. A better approach is to get to know the teacher and find out more about his or her personal and professional agenda. Then listen carefully. Pay special attention to any observations about your child that you hadn't made yourself. Are they valid? Is there room for improvement?

I have been party to an estimated 32 parent-teacher conferences in my life so far, and here is my advice:

1. If you have to preregister for an appointment, scramble to be among the first so that you can get there before work. Unless there is an emergency, noon-time teacher conferences do not make good centerpieces for personal days off.

2. Before you go, ask your child about this teacher. Is she strict? Is she nice to him? Is there anything about her that he especially likes or dislikes? Is she a good teacher? Does he feel he's learning a lot? How does she compare with last year's teacher? You need to be armed with his perspective as well as hers.

3. Essentially, the teacher will tell you whether or not your child is behaving herself and how she is doing in each subject. If he starts glancing at the clock and filling time by talking about the curriculum ("This year we're using cuisinaire rods to teach math concepts"), then it's your turn to talk.

4. What's on your mind? If there's too much homework, if little Charlie has trouble doing it, if discipline seems too lax or punishment too strict, now's the time to speak up.

5. For some reason, teachers rarely volunteer information about something they are uniquely qualified to see: namely, your child's on-site social life. Do the other kids seem to like your Joanie? What does she do at recess? Does she hang with a crowd, and if so, which one? These are all things teachers can tell you, but you usually have to ask.

6. If the teacher has mentioned something in the conference that "needs improvement," as it is euphemistically phrased, ask this question: "How can I help?" In matters academic, social, and chemical, maybe you can help . . . but then, maybe you can't. But just asking the question helps clarify what is your responsibility and what is the teacher's. Maybe you can work as a team on the problem, but maybe the problem is all hers or all yours. In either case, you've shown that you're definitely interested in what's going on at school and you're not lying down on the job as a mom.

"THE TEACHER HATES ME!"

Do you remember, as a child, having a feeling that a teacher just plain didn't like you or didn't really like any of the kids? She liked the boys better, or the goody-goody girls, or the brainy girls, or the kids who sang in the chorus.

In this generation, there's no mention of liking and disliking. Instead, a teacher may claim to have difficulty with your child's learning style. A teacher may be more oriented toward the more motivated children. A teacher may express a preference for the verbally gifted. Some prefer lively questioning minds; some would just as soon the kids all stay quiet and listen. Some like a uniformity of answers in homework; some are looking for and encouraging that special spark.

Because teachers differ so widely, every now and then you will get a teacher who doesn't enjoy teaching your particular, adorable, unique, perfect-in-your-mind little Steve.

When you sense the chemistry isn't working between this teacher and your child, you should certainly inform your principal. You don't want to demand a change except in rare cases, but a forewarning of this kind provides a filter for any bad-chemistry blowup that might happen during the year.

Also, you don't want the principal to assign your child to a similar teacher next year or, worse yet, the same one. Teachers sometimes change grades, too.

A teacher who is a poor fit can make an uncomfortable year for you and your child, but it is probably not a problem that will scar the child for life. A child in school is, in fact, in training to work cooperatively within the system. He is learning both to work together with his peers and to get along with adults other than his parents. Whether the teacher likes him, or vice versa, is not an issue. The teacher's opinion of your parenting, real or perceived, is not an issue.

All that counts is that you think you're in the right school, that you feel you're doing the best you can and are encouraging your child to do the same.

◆ FEELING FUNNY AT SCHOOL

It's easy to see why the whole school thing can make a Jobbed mom insecure. While the experience is crucial and major to the life of your child, it all happens when you're at work.

If you feel out of the loop, one solution is to be proactive at the school. If your schedule has not allowed you to meet your child's new teacher early in the school year, call and make an appointment to chat with her one morning before school starts for the day. Then follow up by sending her notes (which you can drop off at the school office) with questions, concerns, suggestions, and offers of help as needs and opportunities permit.

Be flexible about volunteering when you can, so that you can beg off with a clear conscience when you cannot.

Make friends among the Jobless moms and keep in touch with them, so that major political movements and school gossip get channeled to you. It's easy for them to forget you, simply because you are out of sight and therefore out of mind, so you must be the one to take the first step.

Here are some ideas on how to stay plugged in:

1. Help Jobless moms on weekends. Invite their children over. Jobless moms do not have strong guilt feelings about separation on weekends as we do. Invite the mom to come in for coffee at drop-off or pick-up so you can get to

♦ CAN WE RESCHEDULE? ♦

Some communities are still undergoing a change in which, while the number of Jobbed moms is growing, they are still in the minority. If that's the case with you, be certain that the school knows that 10:30 a.m. coffees and 2 p.m. band concerts are not convenient, but be willing to compromise for activities at 8:30 a.m. and in the evening. If nobody tells the school, they will continue to assume they are dealing with mothers with far more flexible lives.

know each other better. Remember that she may be thinking of you only as a Jobbed mother—so steer the conversation away from your work and onto her life and the school.

2. Carpool a lot on weekends—to birthday parties, Brownie activities, and the Cub Scout camp-out. Don't wait to be asked; just pick up the phone and offer.

3. Sponsor a special outing of your own, even if it's nobody's birthday, to a local park or museum or skating rink. This is an excellent way to get to know your kids' friends. They can be even better at school gossip than the moms are.

4. Volunteer for the class telephone chain, which will give you a good reason to call everyone in the class sooner or later.

Once people get to know you as a person, and vice versa, all the Jobbed and Jobless nonsense will fall away. It's impossible to make gross generalizations about somebody you know and like.

◆ WHEN YOU REALLY SHOULD SHOW UP

As a working mom, you can't go to everything that the school invites you to—or even everything you want to go to. During the work week, there are going to be coffees, concerts, assemblies, parent meetings, field trips, fairs, and sporting events.

As soon as the school calendar arrives in August, you should sit down with your date book and write everything down. Later you can decide what's worth taking time off for.

Which events you should absolutely show up for depends mightily on your schedule, your child, and your school's particular culture. However, certain school events are so meaningful and delightful that you should absolutely try to be there if you possibly can:

1. The first day of school, at least for drop-off and pick-up.

2. The Halloween costume parade, especially in early elementary school.

3. The Christmas concert or play.

4. One field trip during the year, when moms are invited to drive or help, usually in the early elementary years.

5. Any concert, play, assembly, or performance in which your child has a role.

6. The science fair. But do militate for an early morning showing.

7. Field day, if mothers are invited.

8. Parent visiting day, or anything that has the word "parent" or "mother" in the title.

9. If your child competes on a sports team against other schools, you should try to show up at least once during the season. Even big, gruff high school boys play better when their moms are in the bleachers.

10. Graduation or any end-of-year ceremony in which your child has a major role or is being given a prize.

11. The last day of school.

The above list is very flexible. As children grow, they are at first delighted to see their parents at school and then become increasingly embarrassed to see them there. At about the age of 15, most kids would sooner die than have their parents show up anywhere except sporting events and the most intensely parent-oriented events, at which they would be deeply crushed if you didn't show.

When undecided, the litmus test is to ask your children how important your attendance at a particular event will be to them. Explain that you only have so many personal days or vacation days a year and that you get choices, and try to get the children to rate how crucial it is to have you there.

When you absolutely cannot attend, try to send a grandparent or close friend and get pictures or a video. Don't drive yourself nutty with guilt. By the time you've been at a school two or three years, you'll get the hang of which events are critical to attend and which ones even the Jobless moms don't show up for.

PARTING THOUGHT: YOU'RE THE BEST JUDGE

With all else stripped away, your major role at school is to let the teachers know that you care about your children, their education, and their social development and that you stand ready to help.

Beyond that, others have no right to make you feel guilty. You are the best judge of what kind of parent you are. How you see yourself and how well you bring up your children are all that count in the end.

CHAPTER SIX

You Gotta Have Friends

A few years ago, I read about a study in which a hundred men and their wives were each asked to name their best friend.

Ninety percent of the men named their wives.

Eighty percent of the women named . . . another woman.

Like all the best studies, this one proves something that you long suspected. While we are excellent best friends to our husbands, they make terrible best friends for us.

It's not their fault, though. Men tend to base their friendships among themselves on activities like shooting hoops and waxing cars and on lightweight banter like talking about how many megs of RAM they have—plus the classic icebreaker, "How 'bout them Rangers?"

Naturally, if they wanted to talk about anything *deep*, they would turn to a woman. Especially a wife.

Women, on the other hand, base their friendships on an exchange of feelings and emotions, so in times of strain we quite naturally turn to each other.

For another thing, men are *fixers*. Confide a problem to a man, and he will tell you how to fix it. But tell a woman, and she will give you what you really needed in the first place, which was *sympathy*. You just wanted somebody to say "Gosh, that's too bad. You must feel awful." As for fixing the problem, she knows darned well you can do that yourself. For example:

YOU: Gosh, I'm feeling fat today!

YOUR HUSBAND: You *could* lose a few pounds. Why don't you join a gym?

Contrast this with the much more friendly:

YOU: Gosh, I'm feeling fat today!

YOUR REAL BEST FRIEND: You're just feeling that way because it's Monday. I was just thinking you looked pretty svelte.

That's why you need to hang on to woman friends.

The Top Eight Things It Is Totally Pointless to Discuss with a Man

1. Hair and makeup
2. What's new down at Gap Kids
3. The price of your new shoes
4. Friends of his whom you dislike
5. Anything involving female plumbing
6. Little things about him you would change
7. Your previous love life
8. What you should wear tonight

All of these things, however, are instantly intriguing to women. In fact, you could talk about these things more easily to a stranger in a ladies' room than you could to your own husband.

But, of course, the best reason to keep a strong network of woman friends is not to have people to talk to about clothes, but to have friends who will help keep you together emotionally during these difficult years of pressure and duty.

A REALLY GOOD GIRLFRIEND DOES FIVE THINGS

1. Totally accepts what you're saying without being judgmental
2. Helps you decide whether to laugh or cry
3. Expresses empathy and feels with you whatever you feel
4. Offers suggestions for solutions—if you want them
5. Helps you turn melodrama into comedy

◆ THE GIRLFRIENDS ARE THE FIRST TO GO

Ideally, the average woman needs to talk to girlfriends *a couple of times a day*. Back in preagrarian times, women huddled together over their chores all day while the men went out to hunt. The men thought the women were merely pounding skins and chopping meat, but no doubt the women were having ongoing conversations as they worked, about men and babies and the meaning of life.

In our way of life, though, this sort of ongoing huddle just doesn't happen, and the girlfriends are the first to go. If we drew a priority map of our lives, our children, men, and jobs would probably top the list in some varying order, while a whole bunch of other things—our health, our parents, the house, the community, and, yes, the girlfriends—would hover somewhere beneath.

In spite of the time pressure, friendships require work just as marriages do. There are a few magical relationships in which the conversation always picks up just where it left off three years ago, but these are rare. Most of the time, a friend who hasn't heard from you in a while will just assume that you don't care any more.

So the best way to keep someone in your life is to give her attention and reassurance. It doesn't have to take a lot of time. Chances are she doesn't have any more time to receive it than you do to give it.

SEVEN WAYS TO STAY IN TOUCH WITH FRIENDS WHEN THERE JUST DOESN'T SEEM TO BE ANY TIME

1. *Lunch.* The best quality time between women and a time-honored tradition. If you have a singular very good friend you want to see regularly, make it the first Tuesday of every month, or pull out your date book at lunch's end and schedule the next one right away.

2. *Exercise.* Fitness walking is much more fun if you can get a pal to go along.

3. *Breakfast.* If you can squeeze it in after drop-off at school, it's a great way to keep in touch with the mothers of your children's friends as well as with Mothers Who Work Within the Home.

4. *Volunteering.* If you do any sort of volunteer work, at the school or elsewhere, dragoon a friend into joining you. It's much more fun with two and can provide great conversation time.

5. *Letters and notes.* If you're sitting in front of a computer all day professionally, sometimes taking a ten-minute break to dash off a letter to a long-distance friend can be tremendously meaningful to the recipient. Letter-writing is also a thought-provoking alternative to evening television. (Don't expect a reply, though. Letter writing is practically a lost art.)

Notes are a quick way of sending messages of sympathy, congratulations, and thanks. They are faster than phone calls for busy people. If you keep a box of note cards at work and another within easy reach at home—even one in the car if you do any waiting there—you can keep in touch with friends during odd moments during the day.

Postcards work too. While the notion of sending a postcard from a vacation spot is an ancient convention, it makes total sense for working mothers, who have time on vacation that they don't have at any other time. Basically a postcard says, "Hi, I'm alive, we're having fun here in Idaho." But the most important thing it says is "I'm thinking about *you*."

6. *Presents.* Gifts have never been known to hurt a relationship. When time is short, when you're too busy even to exercise some imagination, even some change can buy a little something to signal your thoughtfulness.

No one is too rich or too oversupplied with worldly gifts to ignore a bouquet of flowers, a shell from the beach, a rock from a mountainside, a gift book, a box of good soap. If you're very lucky, you can find a present that's perfect for that particular recipient.

◆ ABOUT PHONE CALLS ◆

1. They don't have to be about anything. They only need to signal "I'm still here; I still care; I'm not in any kind of trouble today; if these kids ever leave home, we'll have lunch."

2. They don't have to be long. If you call often enough, five minutes can be plenty of time to say "Hi."

But even if it's not Perfectly Chosen for Just That Person, even if it's just a General Nice Thing, the fact that you come up with a present of any kind counts for a lot.

7. *The telephone.* When my children were very little and I was fairly house bound and all my friends were in the same boat, we kept in touch with daily phone calls that never involved real questions or plan making but were basically about what everybody was doing that day and how we all felt. The relationships we built were just as strong as if we actually were seeing each other.

In time, we all drifted apart geographically, but the phone calling kept the relationships strong. When all else fails, when it's impossible to actually get together, the phone is a godsend.

◆ THE OLD COLD SHOULDER AND WHEN TO USE IT

Now let's mention an unpleasant hard-and-true fact: You don't really want to keep all your old friends. You know you don't. In friendship, as in all other areas of your life, you have to have priorities.

In every single major life change that we quite naturally undergo—leaving school, getting married, having children, becoming working mothers, moving away—a friend or two is quite naturally shed. Many friendships are based on what you two have in common at any given time. When you have less in common, the friendship may go out the window.

But in this time of our life when time and emotional resources are painfully spare, we must protect ourselves from friendships that spread us too thin. It's an ugly thought, but here are

FOUR FRIENDS WHOM WORKING MOTHERS SHOULD JUST PLAIN DROP

1. *The Resenter.* She was your buddy as long as you had a job and no baby or a baby and no job or until you lost the last of the baby weight. Suddenly, she perceives that you've acquired that one last acquisition, that one extra dollop on your life that she doesn't have on hers, and she's all snarly. Forget her.

2. *The Naysayer.* She lets you talk first, and then takes you apart. Everything good is either too expensive or too fattening. Everybody's out to get her and you. Life is nothing but duty. Who needs this?

3. *The Drainer and Taker.* She pours out her troubles to you, leaving you a soggy sponge, but she's not available to return the favor. She uses you for child care, errands, and assorted favors, but does little in return. Just say no.

4. *The Sloppy Scheduler.* She makes a lunch date, cancels at the last minute, schedules again, cancels again. You get a babysitter so you can have dinner together; she finks out just after the sitter arrives. She casually mentions having you over on Sunday but never calls back to confirm. We all have to be flexible, but you're too busy for this friend.

THE WORKING MOM'S SOCIAL CALENDAR

Snookums is newborn to one year: You catch up with some nonworking friends during maternity leave. You try hard not to become a baby bore who can't talk about anything but Snookums. You are excused from entertaining. You drop any friends who like to stay up late or aren't interested in Snookums.

Snookums is age one to five: Snookums sleeps through the night. You resume lunches with friends at work. People invite you to dinner and you go, dozing off by 10 p.m. You begin to entertain very informally and go out on dates, enjoying the break from Snookums and reveling in the rare treasure of adult conversation. It is hard to relate to people without children.

Snookums is age six to ten: You can stay out as late as 1 a.m. on Friday nights, because Snookums can be bribed to start watching Saturday cartoons without waking you first. You begin driving the kids to Saturday sports and sometimes build a social life around the fellow soccer parents. But you still have time to throw or go to parties. You actively seek out people without children to remind you of what's going on in the rest of the world.

Snookums is age eleven to eighteen: Snookums sleeps later than you do. Attending her now-serious games and competitions may take entire weekends. Now too old for babysitters, either kids are such fun to be with that you include them in all your social events while ignoring your real friends, or they are so untrustworthy that you must stay home with them so they won't burn the house down. Either way, you are not seeing any of your friends. You wonder what grownups are talking about these days.

Snookums turns eighteen: Resume normal social life.

♦ ENTERTAINING
THE WORKING-MOM WAY

There is much that is wonderful about entertaining: having an excuse to dust off the living room, sharing the warm glow of your hearth with old and new friends, laughing late into the night, actually using the wedding presents, the joy of cooking, the whole thing.

When you're a working mother, there is also much that is dismal about entertaining: clearing the toys off the coffee table; trying to cook with a toddler clinging to each knee; spending 12 of your weekly 48 hours off preparing, cooking, and cleaning up when maybe you'd rather be in bed with a good book.

On the other hand, entertaining at home is one of the best ways to ensure that you'll see your friends, especially the couples. Restaurants can be prohibitive for this kind of meeting, and you certainly can't always expect them to invite you over.

But take heart. Everybody knows you don't have any time. And though your working-mom years—averaging 20 for the typical family of 1.5 kids—seem to go on forever, they comprise, in fact, only one fourth of your life. So you're allowed to take two decades off from serious anxiety-producing entertaining.

However, there are ways to entertain in a less trying fashion.

No-Sweat Entertaining Tips for the Working Mom

1. Invite only people you really like and want to see. Don't feel that you must reciprocate invitations just for the sake of reciprocation if this isn't someone you really enjoy. Keep up the acquaintance in other ways, or just stall until you retire.

2. Do not invite your children to the party or allow them to hang around. This is not their playdate, it's yours. Let them come through once and say hello to everybody.

If your children are too young to put themselves to bed, have a neighborhood teenager come in to feed them and sit with them while you cook and entertain. Don't try to do all this yourself.

3. Don't panic and overclean. Pick up the rooms your guests will be using (dining room, living room, bathroom) and close the doors to the rest of them. If someone wants a house tour, pretend you have a child sleeping behind each closed door.

4. For an at-home dinner party, the company is important; the conversation is important; the aura of serenity and charm emanating from the hosts is important. What isn't important is the menu. *How hard something was to make* is not a test of your womanhood. Instead of testing your sanity by making six hard things, try these four simple methods of making an impression:

a) Make six easy things. One main dish and five simple side dishes will fill up the buffet and look like you went to a lot of trouble when all you did was defrost the peas, bake potatoes, open a can of cranberry sauce, toss a salad, buy some fabulous bread, and mold some ice cream.

b) Make either lasagna or paella and serve it with a salad. Period. Everybody loves lasagna, and people are always so relieved to see it instead of rare lamb or warm duck salad or something hopelessly chic. Lasagna requires several bowls and pots in preparation, but it's not what you'd call hard. Paella means some adventurous shopping and a lot of chopping, but it's a one-dish meal, and people always think it's terrifically complicated. Let them think so.

c) Mix homemade dishes with carry-out items or deli stuff. The whole prepared-food explosion was designed for working moms, so why not take advantage of it? I know a working mom who bought her entire Thanksgiving dinner (except the turkey) from a fast food carry-out, threw away the cartons, and served it to a tribe of 20 in-laws. They never knew.

d) If someone offers to bring something (the hors d'oeuvres? the dessert?), let them.

PARTING THOUGHT: FRIENDS AND THE BIG PICTURE

Friends keep you from taking yourself too seriously. Friends help keep your life in perspective. Friends remind you to stop slaving away and have some fun.

A date with a friend forces you to stop what you're doing and consider the world outside your own narrow little life.

CHAPTER SEVEN

Mom on the Job

The last time you saw your coworkers all together before the baby was born was at the baby shower. What a day it was! The presents, the jokes, the well-wishers! The attention! In your excitement, in your normal, necessary prenatal narcissism, it was easy to ignore the emotions and the politics going on elsewhere in the room.

The person designated to take over while you were gone, for example, was more than a little excited about getting her mitts on your job.

Your boss had the good grace *not* to look angry at your departure. He was worried about how he'd manage without you and, at the same time, a teeny bit happy to see how somebody else would do your job differently.

Your best work friends were slightly fearful that you'd never be the same again and would only be able to make baby talk instead of the usual small talk.

Now it's your first day back, and you have just had one of the most earth-shaking experiences of your life: *becoming a parent*. You have been through the amazing miracle of childbirth, you have turned a couple into a family, and the doctor actually trusted you to take the baby home from the hospital, so you must now really be a grownup.

Feeling *transformed*, you walk back into the old place where you used to work. Maybe your coworkers all jump up and throw their arms around you and ask you how you feel and tell you how great it is to see you. But more likely people will sort of look up for a minute and say, "Huh? Oh, did you ever have that baby?'"

So it's a big day for *you* but just another day for the gang at work. Frankly, your departure threw a monkey wrench into the works, and, even if you were gone for only a month, they've since filled in the hole you left.

Your substitute over there is loath to share details of what happened while you were gone because she's decided she wants to keep your job.

Your boss is assuming that you're going to be spending half the day on the phone with the day-care center and that you'll quit before lunch. If not, he's sure that he won't be able to hoodwink you into odd hours and strange duties anymore because your priorities have changed. He sees you as less serious about your work now, *even though all you've done so far is walk in the door,* and he's just waiting for you to prove it.

And your friends know they'll have to put up with one or two Baby Bore stories, but they secretly fear that you'll be sneaking out early every day, leaving the child-free folks with the rest of your work to do.

Now, you're tired, and you're anxious. You have dark circles under your eyes and formula stains on your blouse, but in addition to your list of job duties you have one more thing to do today. You have to prove them all wrong. You have to prove to them that you are not the slightly thick-waisted, baby-crazed, sleep-challenged zombie you appear to be but a much-improved professional who is going to be a better worker from now on.

◆ STAYING CONFIDENT: YES, YOU'RE EVEN BETTER NOW

What you're trying to prove here is that not only are you just as sharp as you were before you had children, you are actually a better worker now. (Or at least you will be when you start getting enough sleep.)

Putting the more neurotic bosses aside, any clear-thinking mature person in authority will tell you he'd hire a working mom over any other kind of applicant for a job that requires clear thinking, organization, and maturity. Here's why:

YOU'RE MORE EFFICIENT NOW

A woman who has a family to go home to is much less likely to prolong a meeting with diversionary amusements, to take a long lunch, to chat with girlfriends on the phone, or to dawdle over her makeup in the ladies' room. She has learned to prioritize her time and get things done at top speed. She's more focused.

A woman who has taken on the ultimate responsibility in parenthood is much less likely to shirk smaller ones. If she can hold her nose and change a diaper, she can hold her nose and take on any number of unpleasant chores and dispatch them in a hurry.

And if a workplace still uses some ancient foot-dragging procedure, chances are it's a working mother who will figure out how to do it faster and better.

You've Got Better People Smarts Now

Being a mother is being a boss, and even the first few months of motherhood teach you how to be a manager and how to manage your manager. (Because what is a baby if not a manager?)

Anybody who has struggled with children through the difficult behavior patterns of toddlerhood and, later, adolescence soon learns that all the previously baffling adults around her are just kids with longer legs.

Most women are intuitive about people, but motherhood gives us enormously useful insights into human behavior and misbehavior. Stubborn staffers, recalcitrant superiors, and querulous clients are all exhibiting childlike symptoms that you can deal with either by using personal experience or by quickly referencing any reliable child development book.

Micromanaging? Whining? Perfectionism? Tardiness? Indecision? Competition? All you need to know you can learn in any kindergarten. And you've learned how to handle it at home.

You Bring More to the Party

In nearly all work situations, the experiences you have on the outside stimulate your thinking and help you to come up with creative ideas. Any and all experience you gain from real life will serve you well on the job.

Let's face it, what do child-free women know about? Make-up. Last night's episode of "Seinfeld." The difference between this Club Med and that Club Med. Whatever they majored in and whatever their job is.

We know all that *plus* the incubation period of chicken pox, how to spell *episiotomy*, the environmental impact of cloth vs. paper diapers, how to handle a wailing baby, how to hire and fire babysitters, how to run an entire household by telephone, and much, much more.

While everybody is entitled to the kind of personal life that allows for outside experiences, working mothers are actually forced into it. Who knows? That hot idea that worked at the nursery school bake sale might easily be translatable into national corporate sales.

You Don't Cry in the Ladies Room Anymore

Remember all the emotional energy that went into your job before you were a mother? All the extracurricular activity—the politicking, the tears, the need for approval, the resentments, the jealousies? Most of that has now been channeled into your family instead. Being a mother is such an enormous emotional commitment that, frankly, emotional issues on the job now look like a hill of beans.

This is the most freeing thing that can happen to you at work. The highs are just as high, but the lows are no big deal.

YOU DON'T FEEL STUCK ANYMORE

Now that you feel so emotionally free on the job and you have this whole other life going on, you can make really rational decisions about whether or not this job is still working for you.

Maybe you're being viewed as half a brain when in fact you feel stronger than ever. Maybe the old job demands don't work with the new hours you must keep. Maybe that person who subbed for you during maternity leave actually succeeded in glomming onto your old job.

The times after the first, or second, or third baby are natural times for women to change job situations or even to start their own businesses, and they do it all the time.

The good part is that when you feel free to walk, it shows. And you are never more valued than when you get that little twinkle in your eye while reading the want ads.

◆ CAREFULLY MUSCLING YOUR WAY BACK IN AT WORK

Okay, so now that you're a working mom, you're a more knowledgeable, more efficient, less political, less weepy sort of employee.

But you cannot just march back to work shouting, "Hey! I'm older and wiser! I'm the improved model! Gimme a corner office and a fat raise!"

Your coworkers would just figure your hormones are still out of balance and bundle you down to medical. And your boss doesn't want to be told. She wants you to prove it.

Try following these guidelines for achieving a smooth reentry back to the ranks of living, working adults.

Do let your boss know when you plan to return from maternity leave. (If you're not sure, make up a likely scenario so he has something to tell the personnel department. But don't leave it wide open.) Remind him of the day of your return at least a week ahead of time. It would be a pretty unattractive surprise for all if they had no place for you to sit or had to send you home because that other woman is still doing your job.

Do dress the part. Motherhood does not mean you have to suddenly start wearing wraparound skirts and cardigan sweaters. Remember, these people already think you're vaguely out of it. So spring for one nifty, new-looking outfit to signal that you haven't been under a rock for nine months. If it has to be a size bigger because you're not back in shape yet, tear out the size tag and forget about it.

Don't plaster baby pictures all over your office, workspace, or cash register, unless that's obviously acceptable in your work culture. Put one small picture on view, but keep that album locked up where even *you* have trouble sneaking peeks at it. Make seriously interested people *beg* to see it.

Don't rattle on about your children even when asked. If your boss or coworker starts to fidget, glaze over, glance at her watch, or pull out her train schedule, you've gone on too long.

Do throw yourself into your work immediately to signal how glad you are to be there (whether you are or not) and that your brain hasn't turned to rice cereal while you were out. Sit down with your sub and demand a list of the new developments in your division. Lunch with your buddies and get the gossip. Make a lot of noise, look busy, blitz out memos.

Don't moan about being tired. You could seem like someone who can't cut the mustard anymore. If you have control over your own workload, don't attempt the hardest things on the days you're most tired.

Don't assume that because your boss is a woman, or even a mother, she is going to understand your motherly needs or the priorities you might have, listen to you talk about your children, or share any of your feelings whatsoever. Women at the top have often made family sacrifices to get there and may not be sympathetic.

Don't think your boss is just going to wave you blissfully out the door when you're close to day-care pickup time. Your goal is to make him forget you have a regularly scheduled departure time. In fact, don't discuss hours unless absolutely necessary. Your boss's priority is *not* your private life but rather the efficient running of his workplace. This is true no matter how much he likes you as a person.

Don't talk about it if you do get a special deal on work hours. Motherhood all by itself does not entitle you to march out on time or early, either regularly or now and then. *Everybody* is entitled to that privilege because everybody has a private life. If the subject ever comes up among your coworkers, that is what you are to say.

Do stick to the deal if you've made one. If you have permission to leave at 5:30 or have promised yourself to do so, be assertive (but quiet) about making it happen every day, so you won't lose the privilege. The ideal is that eventually everybody knows you leave at 5:30 every day, but nobody remembers why.

Don't take a day off every time one of your children sniffles, sneezes, or gets little red spots all over. Of course you'll attend personally to real emergencies. But a mother's presence has never been known to cure the common cold or even the chicken pox. In fact, in young children, knowing that mom will stay home is a very good incentive to feel a little tummy bug coming on.

Do be accepting and understanding if, after a long maternity leave or a long period of working part-time, you find that all those kids you trained, encouraged, and promoted have passed you on the ladder and you end up working for people younger than you are. This is a fact of workplace life for mothers and nonmothers, for men and women both. Remember, you have made this choice, if only subconsciously, and cannot regret it.

◆ SPLAT ON THE GLASS CEILING: THE STICKY PROMOTION STUFF

Time was when women workers were awfully handy to have around to put in rivets and serve hash, but they couldn't get promoted to save their lives.

Things have gotten better . . . but not much. While there may be policies and antidiscrimination laws in place to shatter the glass ceiling, attitude adjustment is moving at a much slower pace. At this time in work history, it is still harder for women to get ahead in most situations than for men, and it is harder for women with children to get ahead than for women without children.

Those working mothers who make it to the top usually design their entire family's lives around their jobs. The desirability and feasibility of doing this depends greatly on what age and kind of children you have, what kind of parents you had, how you feel about motherhood, what kind of husband you have, and what kind of hours and responsibilities are involved in your job. Much depends, too, on your husband's job, your own priorities, your company's culture, and your management's flexibility.

The situation for working mothers on the career ladder will improve:

1. When most men at the top have working-mom wives and understand such women's capabilities and priorities.

2. When the baby boomers, now 31 to 49 years old, begin to retire, leaving fewer experienced heads available for the always-few top jobs. With so many boomers entering the appropriate age for top management at this moment in history, most corporations don't have enough big jobs to go around, and, unfortunately, they can afford to ignore it when experienced employees drop out over quality-of-life issues.

3. When there are people in power, both women and men, who are committed to creating new traditions in flexible, noncompetitive work hours and workplaces. In the meantime, the bigger, newer question is not "Can working mothers get that top job?" but "Do they really want it?" Top-of-the-ladder jobs are still often crafted to suit the lifestyles of men with wives at home, not the lifestyles of women who need wives at home.

For all these reasons, it's probably safe to predict that for the next 20 years working moms will move horizontally much more nimbly and often than they move vertically.

PARTING THOUGHT: BE CHOOSY

To be fulfilled at work, pick and manage your boss carefully, and find a job that makes you happy.

If you find that you're being seen as a lesser asset when you're really twice the woman you used to be, get out of there and go someplace where they appreciate you.

CHAPTER EIGHT

Working Mom vs. the Clock

Once there was a time-efficient working mom—true story!—who every night put her three-year-old in the bathtub with a cheeseburger on a toy boat and read bedtime stories to him while he ate so that she could kill off three evening chores at the same time. Then she dressed him in tomorrow's sweat suit and put him to bed so she wouldn't waste time dressing and undressing him.

While working mothers who hear this story always wonder what happens if the boat capsizes, none of them ever question the necessity of doing two or three things at once.

Funny, isn't it? While very few men would do anything more double-focused than watching a ball game on television and napping at the same time, this sort of time piggybacking comes quite naturally to us moms.

The first rule of working-mom time economics is to do *at least* two things at the same time.

TEN WAYS TO SAVE TIME BY DOING TWO THINGS AT ONCE

1. Commute via car and argue with your mother on the car phone.

2. Cook, clean the kitchen, and return phone calls, using a ten-foot phone cord and a shoulder rest from the telephone store. Yes, the cord will get all tangled, but it's worth it. Alternatively, spring for a cordless phone.

3. Take a shower and rehearse your meeting presentation or your church choir solo.

4. Balance your checkbook and have your hair cut.

5. Paint your nails and watch the news.

6. Commute via bus and do holiday shopping from catalogs.

7. Read a book on the treadmill at the gym.

8. Go power walking and catch up on the gossip with a girlfriend.

9. Watch "Home Improvement" and sew buttons back on shirts.

10. Have a meaningful conversation with your child while walking the dog together.

When you think about it, why does anybody ever do one thing at a time?

◆ BOSSING YOUR TIME AROUND

The easiest thing for working mothers to do in their off hours is to cram in a lot of silly errands and stupid chores. The trouble with this tendency is that even though these activities can be mindless, soothing, and even vaguely pleasurable, they rob you of the opportunity to do big things that are really valuable or fun.

Using the time in your life to do a lot of frittering and pillow plumping instead of speeding through your chores to get to the Stones concert is like using your paycheck to buy five hundred bags of penny candy from the dime store instead of one cashmere sweater.

Keep this in mind: Every working mother, whether she's a waitress or a CEO, is a household executive. And she should manage her time like one.

How do executives use their time? They *only* do the things that *only they* can do. They are paid to have ideas only they can have, make decisions only they can make, execute plans only they have the power to execute. When they are faced with a responsibility that somebody else can handle, they choose, assign, and train somebody else to do it.

That is why you will never find executives making photocopies, licking stamps, emptying the trash, or receiving UPS deliveries at the elevator. The company won't let them do that stuff. For those humongous salaries, they are expected to use their precious time doing only what only they can do.

Think of yourself that way, and get as many stamp-licking-type activities as you can out of your life. (Of course you can't get them all out, but it's something to aspire to.)

Be prepared to give up a little power. If you send your husband to do the grocery shopping instead of going yourself, you will no longer have total control over what is bought. You may have to find a way to use up the salt-free potato chips. (Try crumbling them on a tuna casserole.) But it still beats doing it yourself.

BIG-PICTURE TIME TIPS

1. Delegate everything you possibly can to your husband, your children, or a teenager who can do your errands for you after school, one afternoon a week. Getting someone else to do your grocery shopping, dry cleaning, post office runs, and other errands can save you hours each week.

2. Page through your yellow pages looking for the magic words *Free Delivery*. Whether it's pizza, dry cleaning, groceries, prescription drugs, or video rentals, always try to get someone else to bring it to you.

3. Always order pantyhose through the mail.

4. Leave pithy messages on answering machines instead of playing telephone tag.

5. Using e-mail or writing a note is almost always faster than making a telephone call. Save calls for people you *want* to talk to.

6. Order basic necessities and gifts through mail order as often as possible. Since most catalog goods are not cheap, think about scaling down on the size of the present. It's the thought that counts anyway, right?

Filling out the order form and mailing or faxing it is almost always faster than calling. (Don't you lose patience when the phone clerk gets to the part about the expiration date on your credit card?) Use gift-wrap services when they're not hideously overpriced.

7. Write holiday cards only to out-of-town friends, not to people that you're going to see anyway. Enclose a photocopied newsletter about your family's year (engage only in the most tasteful bragging) instead of scribbling all the news on each card. But do write a brief personal message on each to keep it from looking like a corporate brochure.

8. Order take-out or eat out once a week, no matter how modest the meal.

9. Instead of keeping photo albums, put photos in photo boxes or shoe boxes labeled with the year.

10. Do necessary chores at odd times, when they can be done faster. If you have or can find an old Crock-Pot, load it up at breakfast time and let it cook your dinner all day. At night, when you're not too sleepy to think, lay your work clothes out for the next day—your kids' clothes, too.

11. Don't do everything for your children. As they grow, teach them how to pack their own bags, microwave their own meals, clean the kitchen, keep their books organized, and do the laundry. You not only save time but also fulfill your main job as a parent—to teach your children to be independent.

12. Keep a list of frequently called numbers taped by your phone. Post not just the emergency numbers but also your friends, relatives, kids' friends, pizza parlor, and babysitters. This is much faster than an address book, an electronic organizer, or a Rolodex.

13. Let your standards slip *badly* on the housekeeping front. Do you really need to have all the beds made, even on the days when the photographer from *Martha Stewart Living* is not coming? Do all the drawers and closets have to be maniacally organized? Whenever you find yourself spending more than a one-hour block of time cleaning, take two aspirin and lie down.

14. It is perfectly all right to put off until tomorrow something you are too tired, stressed, or late to do today. Consider this ancient truth: Children will grow faster than you expect. But dishes, ironing, and dust balls are not going anywhere.

15. If your husband complains about dust balls, carry-out from the Taco Bell again, or his unwashed socks, just say, "I *did* get home from work early, and I was going to clean/cook/wash, but I decided to take the kids to the park instead. I think that's more important, don't you?" This works every time.

And finally, avoid at all costs:

THE SEVEN DEADLY TIME WASTERS

1. Nervous snacking. It's not a need for food, it's a need for a soothing rhythmic activity. Unload the dishwasher instead. You know it always needs it.

2. Complaining about how little time you have. Nobody wants to hear it, and you're just venting anyway. Breathe deeply and go back to work.

3. Picking up small plastic objects from the floor. Life is too short. Either get the kids to do it, or shut the door to the room so you don't have to look. Things behind doors don't count.

4. Ironing. Contract it out or wear only no-iron stuff.

5. Tossing and turning at night. Drink warm milk or read a good book. If something is bothering you, write it out in a journal, which will both clarify your thoughts and separate you from your anxieties to some extent.

6. Washing dishes. Get a dishwasher, use paper plates once a week, and, for the inevitable bits, enlist family help. Time yourselves to see how fast you can get it done.

7. Nagging. It quickly becomes an unheard drone and continues because no results accrue. Instead, make quiet, well-reasoned requests, scream briefly for attention, or let it go.

THE LAST WORD ON TIME

As we rush around crazed and loony and late, we occasionally glimpse people who seem to have nothing but time. Toddlers in the playground. Old people on the park bench. Teenagers at the mall. School kids on vacation. Retired folks whacking golf balls or grinning for each other's cameras on bus trips to fun places. Single girls happily dawdling in trendy bars after work.

We see these peaceful people, quietly absorbing energy from each other and the beauty around them and we think, *Where do they get off?*

They are there to remind us that, in the past, we did have time. In the future we will have time. But at the moment we are the busiest we are ever going to be in our whole long lives.

It is good to reflect, now and then, on how rewarding it feels to be *needed*.

PARTING THOUGHT: INDULGE YOURSELF

For the next however-many years, while you are in this time-short period of life, indulge yourself totally in any possible shortcut you can find and afford.

You need it—and deserve it.

CHAPTER NINE

Stressbusting

Taking Time for You

For ten points, answer this multiple-choice question.

The most important thing I bring to my family is:

a) my paycheck

b) my pot roast

c) my proselytizing

d) my peace of mind

Certainly, they like your paycheck and possibly your pot roast. They could live without the proselytizing. But of these things, the greatest gift you give, what will stand them in good stead for life, is your peace of mind.

So now you're saying, "*What* peace of mind?" because this is the most difficult to produce of the four, often because the other three get in the way.

By peace of mind, I mean our sense of satisfaction with our own lives, our balance and self-care, self-esteem, self-love, and all the rest of that *self* stuff.

Without that peace of mind, we are not really capable of giving valuable emotional support to others. Without it, we are prone to various degrees of frustration behavior: spouse abuse, child abuse, drug abuse, alcohol abuse, credit card abuse, that sort of thing. Such angry behavior is about not having rewards in our lives commensurate with the energy we put out.

Now we all know this, but we have a lot of trouble working on the self-esteem project. The reason is that nobody else is responsible for, or interested in, your self-love, and the ones who love you most are very likely to be standing on the other side of the door barking, "Would you *please* finish meditating and come explain this checkbook?" Or "Say, Mom, could you get out of the bathtub and help me find my school shoes?"

It's not that they don't love you. It's just that kids, for example, would much prefer that you drive them to school personally rather than send them on the bus while you squeeze in an aerobics class before work. They may support the idea of your self-love and peace of mind, but it never seems to break at the right time for them.

It's just that everybody is the star of his or her own life story. So please don't forget to be the star of *your* own life story.

♦ THE MID-LIFE VISE

The foundation block for having peace of mind is knowing that the big life decisions you're currently living with fit in with your values. Let's assume you're pretty sure you married the right guy, you're relatively guilt-free about working, the job seems to suit you, you're glad you had children, your house isn't too awful, and your town has not yet filed for bankruptcy.

Even when all that feels right, the years between the ages of, say, 25 to 45 or 30 to 50, when you're a working mother, are going to be absolutely *the most stressful* of your life on a day-to-day basis.

Your parents, your husband, your children, their teachers, their friends, your boss, your employees, your clients, the church, the school, the house, the paper boy, the heating contractor, the plumber, the Maytag repairman, the car, and the dog all require your ministrations, and sometimes they all seem to want it at once.

There is no doubt that you could spend all day every day for 20 years cheering, scolding, reforming, instructing, massaging, and writing notes and checks to these people, institutions, and other assorted creatures.

But you are not going to do that, because it would deplete your energy and make you crabby and useless to everyone and burdensome to many. Pretty soon you'd be putting one of those bumper stickers on your car that says, "Life's a bitch and then you die," which is hardly an inspirational message for your children to see when you pick them up from a birthday party.

You would become unhappy, and, as a wise old philosopher or someone with similar credentials once said, *If Mama ain't happy, ain't nobody happy.*

So even if your true mission in life is to take care of others, even if the greatest satisfaction you can possibly imagine is to be of service to others, you will not be able to fulfill this mission if you don't take some time to care for yourself.

♦ THE ART OF TIME SEIZURE

Once we understand that it is not desirable to be doormats every minute of our lives, we next have to find time to do things for ourselves.

Time, unlike many of life's gifts, is actually issued equally to each of us on a 24-hour-each-day basis. We really do have control of this time, but our lives are littered with gremlins trying to steal the hours.

If you think of each demand on your time as a violent fastball hurtling directly at your head with the intention of literally knocking the life out of you, it will be easy to visualize yourself picking up a big bat and whacking it out into left field.

It's a violent image, sure, but that is sometimes how strongly you have to act in order to seize your time from the greedy clutches of others. Even if you have a husband who says things like "I'll diaper the quints, darling. You just run off and take a walk in the woods by yourself," you can bet that if you answer the phone on the way out it will be your daughter's Brownie leader wanting a dozen cupcakes by tonight.

Time for yourself, clearly, is not just going to fall into your lap. You have to schedule it, protect it, and stick with it, and, if possible, you should aim to do this every single day.

TIME SEIZURE TECHNIQUES

1. Get the children's father to take the kids solely and completely for a few hours on weekends.

Even fathers who swear undying love and devotion can shirk child-care duties because they are afraid they won't know what to do. They can learn the same way you did—by practicing. And they will like it better than they expect. So what if you have to use a sneaky phony method like signing him up to coach the soccer team behind his back? He will thank you for it later.

2. Find self time at the beginning or end of the work day.

Unless you are absolutely tied to your kids' day care or school schedule, why not drop them off early every once in a while and take time for yourself or pause for coffee on the way to picking them up?

3. Take a mental health day, all by yourself or with a friend.

It makes sense to schedule your vacation weeks when the kids are out of school. But think about planning or spontaneously seizing a mental health day off from work when the kids are in school and their father is at work. Spend just one day doing exactly what you want to all day. This technique provides miraculous results. Planning, anticipating, and remembering the day are all delicious.

4. Just say no.

Nobody ever wants to just say "no" when the Cub Scout den mother calls. However, you are now evolved enough to know that, if you are feeling stressed out and homicidal at the moment, it is better for your Cub Scout if you take a bubble bath instead of making cupcakes or driving his den to the fire station open house. Here are some imaginative ways to fend off time thieves:

- "I know somebody who's even better at baking than I am."

- "Is store-bought okay?"
- "I'd like to drive the Scouts, but my driver's license has been temporarily suspended for reckless endangerment. Maybe some other time?"
- "I'm on duty in the emergency room that night."
- "Jury duty."
- "Lyme disease."
- "I'm expecting the linoleum men any minute all this month."
- "I'm sorry, I don't have a child named Jeffrey. You must have the wrong number."
- "Hello? Hello? This is such a bad connection. Give me your number, and I'll call you back."

The key to credible excuse making, of course, is to use only one excuse at a time. If you combine any two excuses, even if they are true, you will sound like you're stretching. Either be firm or be so weird that nobody will want you near their children.

5. Use time-seizure machines and gizmos.

Your watch. Set it five minutes ahead, and you will find yourself with several calm time pockets during the day while you wait for the meeting to start, school to get out, your shift to begin, or your train to arrive.

Your telephone answering machine. Every time the phone rings and you wish it hadn't, let the machine do the work.

Your microwave oven. Really read all the instructions to get the absolute most out of it. Not only is this a machine that will safely cook unattended while you're giving yourself a manicure, but it uses only cooking vessels that can be washed in a dishwasher, thus enabling you to seize pot-scrubbing time for your own personal use.

Your VCR. Used as a babysitter while running a wholesome Disney animated feature, it enables you to capture up to 90 minutes of self time at a crack.

Your pocket calendar and notebook. Simply by writing everything down as it comes to you, you will seize time you would have spent trying to remember it or phoning people to find out. What was the name of that book she suggested you read? Or was it somebody else who suggested it? Who *was* that, anyway?

DE-STRESSING TECHNIQUES

What you do with all the self time you've seized depends entirely on what you like to do and what you can afford. Some working moms train for the marathon, while others lie prone for massages. Some actually cook for pleasure; others would sooner starve.

In case you are so rusty at self time that you need a nudge, here are some ideas:

1. Read a really entertaining or worthwhile book about whatever you're into.

2. Get a facial.

3. Go shopping in all those stores your husband and kids won't let you go to when they're around.

4. Buy yourself something small, useless, and delightful.

5. Have a conversation with a really good girlfriend.

6. Watch television alone with the door closed, and see your favorite show from beginning to end without anybody else channel surfing.

7. Make something.

8. Refinish something.

9. Go to the park or the beach and sit there quietly.

10. Lock yourself in the bathroom with a good magazine for a nice bubble bath.

11. Go for a walk or a bike ride alone.

12. Take a class.

13. Join an amateur sports team.

14. Join an amateur theater group.

15. Join the church choir.

16. Join anything you're interested in.

The point is to have something, whether a moment or an avocation, that is totally, exclusively yours and not bound up with the rest of the family or the job.

And it should be involving enough to remove you emotionally and mentally from whatever is going on in those other two arenas of your life.

◆ HELL WEEK

As a working mother, you know that, if you are assigned a big tight-deadline project at work, whether writing a business plan or catering an event for a passel of big-tipping visiting Japanese businessmen, the following things will automatically happen the very same week:

1. Your husband will go out of town.

2. Your parents will announce that they're passing through town and coming for dinner on Tuesday.

3. Something that you volunteered to do six months ago but forgot about will suddenly come due.

4. One of your kids will get in trouble at school, one will get chicken pox, and one will decide to run for student council.

5. The car will break down.

6. You will suffer a personal injury that is not visible or debilitating but nonetheless painful, such as a pulled back, a mild migraine, or a sprained toe.

7. And—this always happens—*you will get yet another assignment at work.*

Experience has shown that these things tend to run in cycles. There's a crazy cycle in September–October, another all through December, and a third from February to May. If you're a CPA, double March.

My natural reaction to times like this is to eat a lot of chocolate and whine a lot. Both are counterproductive.

Here is a better series of steps to cope with Hell Week stress induced by having too much to do in too short a time:

1. Separate anxiety from activity. When you first realize the horror of your situation, go sit in a quiet room, close your eyes, take ten deep breaths, and then willfully bundle up all your anxiety, panic, and worry and send it off in a mental helium balloon. Contrary to what we often feel, we do not need anxiety to function. It can, in fact, be paralyzing.

2. Write out what you need to do. Using a nice clean sheet of paper (which will give you the illusion of peace and order), write your projects down as topic headings. Then make a list of little steps involved in each project underneath the headings. If you're lucky, you may discover at this point that it's not as bad as you thought.

3. Clean out your life for the next week. Study your calendar and postpone anything you can, canceling the rest. Postpone your teeth-cleaning appointment and lunches with friends (sorry). Cancel that guy who said he was going to clean your rug for free but is actually going to try to sell you a vacuum cleaner. Skip any club and committee meetings that you can. Postpone cleaning and laundry.

4. Delegate. Can somebody else drive to gymnastics just this once? Can a teenage neighbor come over and play video games with the chicken pox kid? Can the deli on the corner cater lasagna and salad for Tuesday night dinner? Can your boss assign you a partner, helper, or extension for your work projects?

5. Assign the remaining chores to time blocks on your calendar. First, write down the fixed appointments and deadlines—the pediatrician, the in-laws' dinner, the project due Wednesday, and the one due Friday. Then find places where it is logical and desirable to do the other steps and write them in on the calendar as appointments with yourself. If you use the odd hours—early mornings, lunch times, late nights—chances are everything will fit.

6. Gather your adrenaline and go. Remind yourself that there are good reasons why you are doing all these things and that it's too bad that they are all happening at once. Remind yourself that you are fortunate indeed to have commitments with work, family, and friends, which is far better than a pitiful life of social isolation and financial disaster. Then get to work.

The 15 minutes you just spent doing these organizational exercises will be your most important 15 of the week. You may have to do Step 1 several times during the week.

Now here's the really mysterious thing about weeks like this: when you are working flat-out, something always gets blessedly canceled. I presume this is because everybody is busy during the same weeks of the year, and your project fell into somebody else's cancellation step. Be grateful.

WHAT NOT TO SKIP DURING TIMES OF STRESS

No matter how bad it gets, try to keep these in your routine:

1. Exercise, even if it's only 20 minutes of brisk walking.

2. Short chats with somebody who makes you laugh.

3. The five basic food groups. You want enduring energy. Sugar highs and alcohol lows are not recommended for now.

4. Bedtime stories or breakfast chats with your children.

5. Washing your hair. Looking bad will make you feel worse.

6. A good night's sleep. Use warm milk or a bedtime book if necessary. Going without sleep will mess up your schedule for the next day.

7. Your sense of humor. All this is temporary—a blip on life's monitor screen.

◆ EMERGENCY SELF TIME ◆

You cannot always know when sudden frustration is going to hit, when your stomach will knot up as you get ready to cry, scream, throw something, or grab a pint of Haagen Daazs and eat it all, one spoonful after another after another.

If you feel it getting that bad, you have permission to do this: *Just stop.*

Put down that pot, get up from that computer, hang up the phone, march out of the mall, leave the kids at the kitchen table, just walk away. Go someplace alone and quiet for 15 minutes by the clock. You will feel better, and chances are nobody will even notice you were gone.

◆ TIME FLIES WHETHER YOU'RE HAVING FUN OR NOT

The hard-pressed life is really made up of little decisions. You *can* have it all, but you cannot have it *all at once.*

For example, you've experienced that moment, at the end of a long hard day, when the kids are finally in bed and you've got half an hour until your own bedtime. Should you:

1. Work on the income taxes?

2. Or climb into bed under a fat quilt with a great novel?

Sometimes you have to choose the thing you absolutely must do sooner or later. Sometimes you haven't the strength to even struggle with it, and then it's better to just collapse in a heap. When it comes to choices of what to do with time, though, there is one thought that helps me, and it is this:

If you don't have some fun today, God isn't going to give you another day at the end of your life to make up for it.

PARTING THOUGHT:
BE GOOD TO YOURSELF

Your years as a working mother with children at home are among the busiest, the hardest, and the most fun of your life. You actually draw strength and stability from the many roles in your life.

But amid all the demands, try to single out some things that will reward and satisfy you. Be good to yourself, and all the rest will follow.

◆ ◆ ◆

For Balancing Work and Family—
Peterson's Can Help!

The Working Parents Help Book
Susan Crites Price and Tom Price
Organized in problem and solution format,
it provides strategies to help working
parents cope with ongoing issues.
ISBN 1-56079-333-3, 285 pp., 9 x 7, $12.95 pb

The Three-Career Couple
Her Job, His Job, and Their "Job"
Together
Marcia Byalick and Linda Saslow
Supportive and lively, it draws on the everyday
challenges faced by working couples and offers
hope laced with humor.
ISBN 1-56079-239-6, 248 pp., 6 x 9, $12.95 pb

100 Things You Can Do
to Keep Your Family Together
When It Sometimes Seems Like the
Whole World is Trying to Pull it Apart
Marge Kennedy
Filled with suggestions about ways to
enhance family togetherness, this book
is practical, realistic, and fun.
ISBN 1-56079-340-6, 112 pp., 9 x 6, $5.95 pb

Are Our Kids All Right?
Answers to the Tough Questions
About Child Care Today
Susan Dynerman
Helps parents make informed decisions by
exploring the impact of different child-care
arrangements on children.
ISBN 1-56079-334-1, 384 pp., 6 x 9, $19.95 hc

How Come I Feel So Disconnected
If This is Such A User-Friendly World?
Reconnecting with Your Family, Friends
. . . and Your Life
Marcia Byalick and Linda Saslow
Includes dozens of thought-provoking ideas
of things we can do right now to reconnect
with family, friends, and ourselves.
ISBN 1-56079-395-3, 208 pp., 8 x 8, $9.95 pb

Good Enough Mothers
Changing Expectations for Ourselves
Melinda M. Marshall
Examines the tradeoffs working mothers
must make in order to achieve balance
and fulfillment in their lives.
ISBN 1-56079-253-1, 344 pp., 6 x 9,
$18.95 hc; ISBN 1-56079-433-X, $10.95 pb

To Order Call 800-338-3282
Or—Fax: Attn. Customer Service—609-243-9150

Ⓟ **Peterson's**
Princeton, NJ